Jame̶̶̶̶ ̶i̶n

no name in the street

James Baldwin was born in 1924 and educated in New York. He is the author of more than twenty works of fiction and nonfiction, including *Go Tell It on the Mountain*; *Notes of a Native Son*; *Giovanni's Room*; *Nobody Knows My Name*; *Another Country*; *The Fire Next Time*; *Nothing Personal*; *Blues for Mister Charlie*; *Going to Meet the Man*; *The Amen Corner*; *Tell Me How Long the Train's Been Gone*; *One Day When I Was Lost*; *If Beale Street Could Talk*; *The Devil Finds Work*; *Little Man, Little Man*; *Just Above My Head*; *The Evidence of Things Not Seen*; *Jimmy's Blues*; and *The Price of the Ticket*. Among the awards he received are a Eugene F. Saxon Memorial Trust Award, a Rosenwald Fellowship, a Guggenheim Fellowship, a *Partisan Review* Fellowship, and a Ford Foundation grant. He was made a Commander of the Legion of Honor in 1986. He died in 1987.

INTERNATIONAL

no name in the street

James Baldwin

Vintage International
Vintage Books
A Division of Random House, Inc.
New York

FIRST VINTAGE INTERNATIONAL EDITION, JANUARY 2007

Copyright © 1972 by James Baldwin,
copyright renewed 2000 by Gloria Baldwin Karefa-Smart

Vintage is a registered trademark and Vintage International and
colophon are trademarks of Random House, Inc.

Cataloging-in-Publication Data is on file at the Library of Congress.

Vintage ISBN: 978-0-307-27592-9

Book design by Lynn Braswell, Bob Korn, and Steve Walker

www.vintagebooks.com

Printed in the United States of America
20 19 18 17 16 15

for

Berdis Baldwin
and
Beauford DeLaney
and
Rudy Lombard
and
Jerome

His remembrance
shall perish from the earth
and He shall have
no name in the street.
He shall be driven from light
into darkness,
and chased out of the world.

Job 18:17–18

If I had-a- my way
I'd tear this building down.
Great God, then, if I had-a- my way
If I had-a- my way, little children,
I'd tear this building down.

> —Slave Song

Just a little while to stay here,
Just a little while to stay.

> —Traditional

take me to the water

"That *is* a good idea," I heard my mother say. She was staring at a wad of black velvet, which she held in her hand, and she carefully placed this bit of cloth in a closet. We can guess how old I must have been from the fact that for years afterward I thought that an "idea" was a piece of black velvet.

Much, much, much has been blotted out, coming back only lately in bewildering and untrustworthy flashes. I must have been about five, I should think, when I made my connection between ideas and velvet, but I may have been younger; this may have been the same year that my father had me circumcised, a terrifying event which I scarcely remember at all; or I may think I was five because I remember tugging at my mother's skirts once and watching her face while she was telling someone else that she was twenty-seven. This meant, for me, that she was virtually in the grave already, and I tugged a little harder at her skirts. I already knew, for some reason, or had given myself some reason to believe, that she had been twenty-two when I was born. And, though I can't count today, I could count when I was little.

I was the only child in the house—or houses—for a while, a halcyon period which memory has quite repudiated; and if I remember myself as tugging at my mother's skirts and staring up into her face, it was because I was so terrified of the man we called my father; who did not arrive on *my* scene, really, until I was more than two years old. I have written both too much and too little about this man, whom I did not understand till he was past understanding. In my first memory of him, he is standing in the kitchen, drying the dishes. My mother had dressed me to go out, she is taking me someplace, and it must be winter, because I am wearing, in my memory, one of those cloth hats with a kind of visor, which button under the chin—a Lindbergh hat, I think. I am apparently in my mother's arms, for I am staring at my father over my mother's shoulder, we are near the door; and my father smiles. This may be a memory, I think it is, but it may be a fantasy. One of the very last times I saw my father on his feet, I was staring at him over my mother's shoulder—she had come rushing into the room to separate us—and my father was not smiling and neither was I.

His mother, Barbara, lived in our house, and she had been born in slavery. She was so old that she never moved from her bed. I remember her as pale and gaunt and she must have worn a kerchief because I don't remember her hair. I remember that she loved me; she used to scold her son about the way he treated me; and he was a little afraid of her. When she died, she called me into the room to give me a present—one of those old, round, metal boxes, usually with a floral design, used for candy. *She* thought it was full of candy and *I* thought it was full of candy, but it wasn't. After she died, I opened it and it was full of needles and thread.

This broke my heart, of course, but her going broke

so I will not say that children love miracles, but I will say that I think we did. A newborn baby is an extraordinary event; and I have never seen two babies who looked or even sounded remotely alike. Here it is, this breathing miracle who could not live an instant without you, with a skull more fragile than an egg, a miracle of eyes, legs, toenails, and (especially) lungs. It gropes in the light like a blind thing—it *is,* for the moment, blind—what can it make of what it sees? It's got a little hair, which it's going to lose, it's got no teeth, it pees all over you, it belches, and when it's frightened or hungry, quite without knowing what a miracle it's accomplishing, it exercises its lungs. You watch it discover it has a hand; then it discovers it has toes. Presently, it discovers it has *you,* and since it has already decided it wants to live, it gives you a toothless smile when you come near it, gurgles or giggles when you pick it up, holds you tight by the thumb or the eyeball or the hair, and, having already opted against solitude, howls when you put it down. You begin the extraordinary journey of beginning to know and to control this creature. You know the sound—the meaning—of one cry from another; without knowing that you know it. You know when it's hungry—that's one sound. You know when it's wet—that's another sound. You know when it's angry. You know when it's bored. You know when it's frightened. You know when it's suffering. You come or you go or you sit still according to the sound the baby makes. And you watch over it where I was born, even in your sleep, because rats love the odor of newborn babies and are much, much bigger.

By the time it has managed to crawl under every bed, nearly suffocate itself in every drawer, nearly strangle itself with string, somehow, God knows how, trapped itself behind the radiator, been pulled back, by one leg, from its suicidal investigation of the staircase, and nearly poisoned itself with everything—*its* hand being quicker than *your* eye—it can possibly get into its mouth, you have either grown to love it or you have left home.

I, James, in August. George, in January. Barbara, in August. Wilmer, in October, David, in December. Gloria, Ruth, Elizabeth, and (when we thought it was over!) Paula Maria, named by me, born on the day our father died, all in the summertime.

The youngest son of the New Orleans branch of the family—family, here, is used loosely and has to be; we knew almost nothing about this branch, which knew nothing about us; Daddy, the great good friend of the Great God Almighty, had simply fled the South, leaving a branch behind. As I have said, he was the son of a slave, and his youngest daughter, by his first marriage, is my mother's age and his youngest son is nine years older than I. This boy, who did not get along with his father, was my elder brother, as far as I then knew, and he sometimes took me with him here and there. He took me into the Coney Island breakers on his back one day, teaching me to swim, and somehow ducked beneath me, playing, or was carried away from me for a moment, terrified, caught me and brought me above the waves. In the time that his body vanished beneath me and the waters rolled over my head, I still remember the slimy sea water and the blinding green —it was not green; it was all the world's snot and vomit; it entered into me; when my head was abruptly lifted out of the water, when I felt my brother's arms and saw his worried face—his eyes looking steadily into mine with the intense and yet impersonal anxiety of a surgeon, the sky above me not yet in focus, my lungs failing to deliver the mighty scream I had nearly burst with in the depths, my four or five or six-year-old legs kicking—and my brother slung me over his shoulder like a piece of meat, or a much beloved child, and strode up out of the sea with me, with me! he had saved me, after all, I learned something about the terror and the loneliness and the depth and the height of love.

Not so very much later, this brother, who was in his teens, fooling around with girls or shooting dice with his friends, who knows, came home late, which was forbidden in our Baptist house, and had a terrible fight with his Daddy and left the house and never came back. He swore that he never would come back, that his Daddy would never see him again. And he never did come back, not while Daddy was still alive. Daddy wrote, but his son never answered. When I became a young minister, I was asked to write him, and I did— sometimes my father dictated the letters to me. And the boy answered me, sometimes, but he never answered his father and never mentioned him. Daddy slowly began to realize that he was never going to see that son, who was his darling, the apple of his eye, anymore, and this broke his heart and destroyed his will and helped him into the madhouse and the grave —my only intimation, perhaps, during all those years, that he was human. The son came home, when his father died, to help me bury him. Then he went away again, and I didn't see him until I had to go to California on a Civil Rights gig, and he met me at the airport. By then, I was thirty-nine and he was nearly fifty, I had made his disowned father's name famous, and I had left home in exactly the same way he did, for more or less the same reasons, and when I was seventeen.

Since Martin's death, in Memphis, and that tremendous day in Atlanta, something has altered in me, something has gone away. Perhaps even more than the death itself, the manner of his death has forced me into a judgment concerning human life and human beings which I have always been reluctant to make— indeed, I can see that a great deal of what the knowledgeable would call my life-style is dictated by this reluctance. Incontestably, alas, most people are not, in action, worth very much; and yet, every human being is an unprecedented miracle. One tries to treat them as the miracles they are, while trying to protect oneself against the disasters they've become. This is not very different from the act of faith demanded by all those marches and petitions while Martin was still alive. One could scarcely be deluded by Americans anymore, one scarcely dared expect anything from the great, vast, blank generality; and yet one was compelled to demand of Americans—and for their sakes, after all—a generosity, a clarity, and a nobility which they did not dream of demanding of themselves. Part of the error was irreducible, in that the marchers and petitioners were forced to suppose the existence of an entity which, when the chips were down, could not be located—*i.e.*, there *are* no American people yet: but to this speculation (or desperate hope) we shall presently return. Perhaps, however, the moral of the story (and the hope of the world) lies in what one demands, not of others, but of oneself. However that may be, the failure and the betrayal are in the record book forever, and sum up, and condemn, forever, those descendants of a barbarous Europe who arbitrarily and arrogantly reserve the right to call themselves Americans.

The mind is a strange and terrible vehicle, moving according to rigorous rules of its own; and my own mind, after I had left Atlanta, began to move backward in time, to places, people, and events I thought I had forgotten. Sorrow drove it there, I think, sorrow, and a certain kind of bewilderment, triggered, perhaps, by something which happened to me in connection with Martin's funeral.

When Martin was murdered, I was based in Hollywood, working—working, in fact, on the screen version of *The Autobiography of Malcolm X.* This was a difficult assignment, since I had known Malcolm, after all, crossed swords with him, worked with him, and held him in that great esteem which is not easily distinguishable, if it is distinguishable at all, from love. (The Hollywood gig did not work out because I did not wish to be a party to a second assassination: but we will also return to Hollywood, presently.)

Very shortly before his death, I had to appear with Martin at Carnegie Hall, in New York. Having been on the Coast so long, I had nothing suitable to wear for my Carnegie Hall gig, and so I rushed out, got a dark suit, got it fitted, and made my appearance. Something like two weeks later, I wore this same suit to Martin's funeral; returned to Hollywood; presently, had to come East again, on business. I ran into Leonard Lyons one night, and I told him that I would never be able to wear that suit again. Leonard put this in his column. I went back to Hollywood.

Weeks later, either because of a Civil Rights obligation, or because of Columbia Pictures, I was back in New York. On my desk in New York were various messages—and it must be said that my sister, Gloria, who worked for me then, is extremely selective, not to say brutal, about the messages she leaves on my desk. I don't see, simply, most of the messages I get. I couldn't conceivably live with them. No one could—as Gloria knows. However, my best friend, black, when I had been in junior high school, when I was twelve or thirteen, had been calling and calling and calling. The guilt of the survivor is a real guilt—as I was now to discover. In a way that I may never be able to make real for my countrymen, or myself, the fact that I had "made it"—that is, had been seen on television, and at Sardi's, could (presumably!) sign a check anywhere in the world, could, in short, for the length of an entrance, a dinner, or a drink, intimidate headwaiters by the use of a name which had not been mine when I was born and which love had compelled me to make my own—meant that I had betrayed the people who had produced me. Nothing could be more unutterably paradoxical: to have thrown in your lap what you never dreamed of getting, and, in sober, bitter truth, could never have dreamed of having, and that at the price of an assumed betrayal of your brothers and your sisters! One is always disproving the accusation in action as futile as it is inevitable.

I had not seen this friend—who could scarcely, any longer, be called a friend—in many years. I was brighter, or more driven than he—not my fault!—and, though neither of us knew it then, our friendship really ended during my ministry and was deader than my hope of heaven by the time I left the pulpit, the church, and home. Hindsight indicates, obviously, that this particular rupture, which was, of necessity, exceedingly brutal and which involved, after all, the deliberate repudiation of everything and everyone that had given me an identity until that moment, must have left some scars. The current of my life meant that I did not see this person very often, but I was always terribly guilty when I did. I was guilty because I had nothing to say to him, and at one time I had told him everything, or nearly everything. I was guilty because he was just another post-office worker, and we had dreamed such tremendous futures for ourselves. I was guilty because he and his family had been very nice to me during an awful time in my life and now none of that meant anything to me. I was guilty because I knew, at the bottom of my heart, that I judged this unremarkable colored man very harshly, far more harshly than I would have done if he were white, and I knew this to be unjust as well as sinister. I was furious because he thought my life was easy and I thought my life was hard, and I yet had to see that by his lights, certainly, and by any ordinary yardstick, my life was enviable compared to his. And if, as I kept saying, it was not my fault, it was not *his* fault, either. You can certainly see why I tended to avoid my old school chum.

But I called him, of course. I thought that he probably needed money, because that was the only thing, by now, that I could possibly hope to give him. But, no.

He, or his wife, or a relative, had read the Leonard Lyons column and knew that I had a suit I wasn't wearing, and—as he remembered in one way and I in quite another—he was just my size.

Now, for me, that suit was drenched in the blood of all the crimes of my country. If I had said to Leonard, somewhat melodramatically, no doubt, that I could never wear it again, I was, just the same, being honest. I simply could not put it on, or look at it, without thinking of Martin, and Martin's end, of what he had meant to me, and to so many. I could not put it on without a bleak, pale, cold wonder about the future. I could not, in short, live with it, it was too heavy a garment. Yet—it was only a suit, worn, at most, three times. It was not a very expensive suit, but it was still more expensive than any my friend could buy. He could not afford to have suits in his closet which he didn't wear, he couldn't afford to throw suits away— he couldn't, in short, afford my elegant despair. Martin was dead, but *he* was living, he needed a suit, and —I was just his size. He invited me for dinner that evening, and I said that I would bring him the suit.

The American situation being what it is, and American taxi drivers being what they mostly are, I have, in effect, been forbidden to expose myself to the quite tremendous hazards of getting a cab to stop for me in New York, and have been forced to hire cars. Naturally, the car which picked me up on that particular guilty evening was a Cadillac limousine about seventy-three blocks long, and, naturally, the chauffeur was white. Neither did he want to drive a black man through Harlem to the Bronx, but American democracy has always been at the mercy of the dollar: the chauffeur may not have liked the gig, but he certainly wasn't about to lose the bread. Here we were, then, this terrified white man and myself, trapped in this leviathan, eyed bitterly, as it passed, by a totally hostile population. But it was not the chauffeur which the population looked on with such wry contempt: I held the suit over my arm, and was tempted to wave it: *I'm only taking a suit to a friend!*

I knew how they felt about black men in limousines —unless they were popular idols—and I couldn't blame them, and I knew that I could never explain. We found the house, and, with the suit over my arm, I mounted the familiar stairs.

I was no longer the person my friend and his family had known and loved—I was a stranger now, and keenly aware of it, and trying hard to act, as it were, normal. But nothing *can* be normal in such a situation. They *had* known me, and they *had* loved me; but now they couldn't be blamed for feeling *He thinks he's too good for us now.* I certainly didn't feel that, but I had no conceivable relationship to them anymore—that shy, pop-eyed thirteen year old my friend's mother had scolded and loved was no more. *I* was not the same, but *they* were, as though they had been trapped, preserved, in that moment in time. They seemed scarcely to have grown any older, my friend and his mother, and they greeted me as they had greeted me years ago, though I was now well past forty and felt every hour of it. My friend and I remained alike only in that neither of us had gained any weight. His face was as boyish as ever, and his voice; only a touch of grey in his hair proved that we were no longer at P.S. 139. And my life came with me into their small, dark, unspeakably respectable, incredibly hard-won rooms like the roar of champagne and the odor of brimstone. They still believed in the Lord, but I had quarreled with Him, and offended Him, and walked out of His house. They didn't smoke, but they knew (from seeing me on television) that I did, and they had placed about the room, in deference to me, those hideous little ash trays which can hold exactly one cigarette butt. And there was a bottle of whiskey, too, and they asked me if I wanted steak or chicken; for, in my travels, I might have learned not to like fried chicken anymore. I said, much relieved to be able to tell the truth, that I preferred chicken. I gave my friend the suit.

My friend's stepdaughter is young, considers herself a militant, and we had a brief argument concerning Bill Styron's *Nat Turner*, which I suggested that she read before condemning. This rather shocked the child, whose militancy, like that of many, tends to be a matter of indigestible fury and slogans and quotations. It rather checked the company, which had not imagined that I and a black militant could possibly disagree about anything. But what was most striking about our brief exchange was that it obliquely revealed how little the girl respected her stepfather. She appeared not to respect him at all. This was not revealed by anything she said to him, but by the fact that she said nothing to him. She barely looked at him. He didn't count.

I always think that this is a terrible thing to happen to a man, especially in his own house, and I am always terribly humiliated for the man to whom it happens. Then, of course, you get angry at the man for allowing it to happen.

And *how* had it happened? He had never been the brightest boy in the world, nobody is, but he had been energetic, active, funny, wrestling, playing handball, cheerfully submitting to being tyrannized by me, even to the extent of kneeling before the altar and having his soul saved—my insistence had accomplished that. I looked at him and remembered his sweating and beautiful face that night as he wrestled on the church floor and we prayed him through. I remembered his older brother, who had died in Sicily, in battle for the free world—he had barely had time to see Sicily before he died and had assuredly never seen the free world. I remembered the day he came to see me to tell me that his sister, who had been very ill, had died. We sat on the steps of the tenement, he was looking down as he told me, one finger making a circle on the step, and his tears splashed on the wood. We were children then, his sister had not been much older, and he was the youngest and now the only boy. But this was not *how* it had happened, although I thought I could see, watching his widowed mother's still very handsome face watching him, how her human need might have held and trapped and frozen him. She had been sewing in the garment center all the years I knew them, rushing home to get supper on the table before her husband got home from *his* job; at night, and on Sundays, he was a deacon; and God knows, or should, where his energy came from. When I began working for the garment center, I used to see her, from time to time, rushing to catch the bus, in a crowd of black and Puerto Rican ladies.

And, yes, we had all loved each other then, and I had had great respect for my friend, who was handsomer than I, and more athletic, and more popular, and who beat me in every game I was foolish enough to play with him. I had gone my way and life had accomplished its inexorable mathematic—and what in the world was I by now but an aging, lonely, sexually dubious, politically outrageous, unspeakably erratic freak? his old friend. And what was *he* now? he worked for the post office and was building a house next door to his mother, in, I think, Long Island. They, too, then, had made it. But what I could not understand was how nothing seemed to have touched this man. We are living through what our church described as "these last and evil days," through wars and rumors of wars, to say the least. He could, for example, have known something about the anti-poverty program if only because his wife was more or less involved in it. He should have known something about the then raging school battle, if only because his stepdaughter was a student; and she, whether or not she had thought her position through, was certainly involved. She may have hoped, at one time, anyway, for his clarity and his help. But, no. He seemed as little touched by the cataclysm in his house and all around him as he was by the mail he handled every day. I found this unbelievable, and, given my temperament and our old connection, maddening. We got into a battle about the war in Vietnam. I probably really should not have allowed this to happen, but it was partly the stepdaughter's prodding. And I was astounded that my friend would defend this particular racist folly. What for? for his job at the post office? And the answer came back at once, alas—yes. For his job at the post office. I told him that Americans had no business at all in Vietnam; and that black people certainly had no business there, aiding the slave master to enslave yet more millions of dark people, and also identifying themselves with the white American crimes: we, the blacks, are going to need our allies, for the Americans, odd as it may sound at the moment, will presently have none. It wasn't, I said, hard to understand why a black boy, standing, futureless, on the corner, would decide to join the Army, nor was it hard to decipher the slave master's reasons for hoping that he wouldn't live to come home, with a gun; but it wasn't necessary, after all, to defend it: to defend, that is, one's murder and one's murderers. "Wait a minute," he said, "let me stand up and tell you what I think we're trying to do there." *"We?"* I cried, "what motherfucking *we?* You stand up, motherfucker, and I'll kick you in the ass!"

He looked at me. His mother conveyed—but the good Lord knows I had hurt her—that she didn't want that language in her house, and that I had never talked that way before. And I love the lady. I had meant no disrespect. I stared at my friend, my old friend, and felt millions of people staring at us both. I tried to make a kind of joke out of it all. But it was too late. The way they looked at me proved that I had tipped my hand. And *this* hurt *me.* They should have known me better, or at least enough, to have known that I meant what I said. But the general reaction to famous people who hold difficult opinions is that they can't really mean it. It's considered, generally, to be merely an astute way of attracting public attention, a way of making oneself interesting: one marches in Montgomery, for example, merely (in my own case) to sell one's books. Well. There is nothing, then, to be said. There went the friendly fried chicken dinner. There went the loving past. I watched the mother watching me, wondering what had happened to her beloved Jimmy, and giving me up: her sourest suspicions confirmed. In great weariness I poured myself yet another stiff drink, by now definitively condemned, and lit another cigarette, they watching me all the while for symptoms of cancer, and with a precipice at my feet.

For that bloody suit was *their* suit, after all, it had been bought *for* them, it had even been bought *by* them: *they* had created Martin, he had not created them, and the blood in which the fabric of that suit was stiffening was theirs. The distance between us, and I had never thought of this before, was that they did not know this, and I now dared to realize that I loved them more than they loved me. And I do not mean that my love was greater: who dares judge the inexpressible expense another pays for his life? who knows how much one is loved, by whom, or what that love may be called on to do? No, the way the cards had fallen meant that I had to face more about them than they could know about me, knew their rent, whereas they did not know.mine, and was condemned to make them uncomfortable. For, on the other hand, they certainly wanted that freedom which they thought was mine— that frightening limousine, for example, or the power to give away a suit, or my increasingly terrifying trans-Atlantic journeys. How can one say that freedom is taken, not given, and that no one is free until all are free? and that the price is high.

My friend tried on the suit, a perfect fit, and they all admired him in it, and I went home.

————————

Well. Time passes and passes. It passes backward and it passes forward and it carries you along, and no one in the whole wide world knows more about time than this: it is carrying you through an element you do not understand into an element you will not remember. Yet, *something* remembers—it can even be said that something avenges: the trap of our century, and the subject now before us.

I left home—Harlem—in 1942. I returned, in 1946, to do, with a white photographer, one of several unpublished efforts; had planned to marry, then realized that I couldn't—or shouldn't, which comes to the same thing—threw my wedding rings into the Hudson River, and left New York for Paris, in 1948. By this time, of course, I was mad, as mad as my dead father. If I had not gone mad, I could not have left.

I starved in Paris for a while, but I learned something: for one thing, I fell in love. Or, more accurately, I realized, and accepted for the first time that love was not merely a general, human possibility, nor merely the disaster it had so often, by then, been for me—according to me—nor was it something that happened to other people, like death, nor was it merely a mortal danger: it was among *my* possibilities, for here it was, breathing and belching beside me, and it was the key to life. Not merely the key to *my* life, but to life itself.

bles—and, in Paris, *les misérables* are Algerian. They slept four or five or six to a room, and they slept in shifts, they were treated like dirt, and they scraped such sustenance as they could off the filthy, unyielding Paris stones. The French called them lazy because they appeared to spend most of their time sitting around, drinking tea, in their cafés. But they were not lazy. They were mostly unable to find work, and their rooms were freezing. (French students spent most of their time in cafés, too, for the same reason, but no one called them lazy.) The Arab cafés were warm and cheap, and they were together there. They could not, in the main, afford the French cafés, nor in the main, were they welcome there. And, though they spoke French, and had been, in a sense, produced by France, they were not at home in Paris, no more at home than I, though for a different reason. They remembered, as it were, an opulence, opulence of taste, touch, water, sun, which I had barely dreamed of, and they had not come to France to stay. One day they were going home, and they knew exactly where home was. They, thus, held something within them which they would never surrender to France. But on my side of the ocean, or so it seemed to me then, we had surrendered everything, or had had everything taken away, and there was no place for us to go: we *were* home. The Arabs were together in Paris, but the American blacks were alone. The Algerian poverty was absolute, their stratagems grim, their personalities, for me, unreadable, their present bloody and their future certain to be more so: and yet, after all, their situation was far more coherent than mine. I will not say that I envied them, for I didn't, and the directness of their hunger, or hungers, intimidated me; but I respected them, and as I began to discern what their history had made of them, I began to suspect, somewhat painfully, what my history had made of me.

The French were still hopelessly slugging it out in Indo-China when I first arrived in France, and I was living in Paris when Dien Bien Phu fell. The Algerian rug-sellers and peanut vendors on the streets of Paris then had obviously not the remotest connection with this most crucial of the French reverses; and yet the attitude of the police, which had always been menacing, began to be yet more snide and vindictive. This puzzled me at first, but it shouldn't have. This is the way people react to the loss of empire—for the loss of an empire also implies a radical revision of the individual identity—and I was to see this over and over again, not only in France. The Arabs were not a part of Indo-China, but they *were* part of an empire visibly and swiftly crumbling, and part of a history which was achieving, in the most literal and frightening sense, its *dénouement*—was revealing itself, that is, as being not at all the myth which the French had made of it—and the French authority to rule over them was being more hotly contested with every hour. The challenged authority, unable to justify itself and not dreaming indeed of even attempting to do so, simply increased its force. This had the interesting result of revealing how frightened the French authority had become, and many a North African then resolved, *coûte que coûte,* to bring the French to another Dien Bien Phu.

Something else struck me, which I was to watch more closely in my own country. The French were hurt and furious that their stewardship should be questioned, especially by those they ruled, and if, in this, they were not very original, they were exceedingly intense. After all, as they continually pointed out, there had been nothing in those colonies before they got there, nothing at all; or what meagre resources of mineral or oil there might have been weren't doing the natives any good because the natives didn't even know that they were there, or what they were there for. Thus, the exploitation of the colony's resources was done for the good of the natives; and so vocal could the French become as concerns what they had brought into their colonies that it would have been the height of bad manners to have asked what they had brought out. (I was later to see something of how this fair exchange worked when I visited Senegal and Guinea.)

It was strange to find oneself, in another language, in another country, listening to the same old song and hearing oneself condemned in the same old way. The French (for example) had always had excellent relations with their natives, and they had a treasurehouse of anecdotes to prove it. (I never found any natives to corroborate the anecdotes, but, then, I have never met an African who did not loathe Dr. Schweitzer.) They cited the hospitals built, and the schools—I was to see some of these later, too. Every once in a while someone might be made uneasy by the color of my skin, or an expression on my face, or I might say something to make him uneasy, or I might, arbitrarily (there was no reason to suppose that they wanted me), claim kinship with the Arabs. Then, I was told, with a generous smile, that I was different: *le noir Americain est très évolué, voyons!* But the Arabs were not like me, they were not "civilized" like me. It was something of a shock to hear myself described as civilized, but the accolade thirsted for so long had, alas, been delivered too late, and I was fascinated by one of several inconsistencies. I have never heard a Frenchman describe the United States as civilized, not even those Frenchmen who like the States. Of course, I think the truth is that the French do not consider that the world contains any nation as civilized as France. But, leaving that aside, if so crude a nation as the United States could produce so gloriously civilized a creature as myself, how was it that the French, armed with centuries of civilized grace, had been unable to civilize the Arab? I thought that this was a very cunning question, but I was wrong, because the answer was so simple: the Arabs did not wish to be civilized. Oh, it was not possible for an American to understand these people as the French did; after all,

27

they had got on well together for nearly one hundred and thirty years. But they had, the Arabs, their customs, their dialects, languages, tribes, regions, another religion, or, perhaps, many religions—and the French were not *raciste*, like the Americans, they did not believe in destroying indigenous cultures. And then, too, the Arab was always hiding something; you couldn't guess what he was thinking and couldn't trust what he was saying. And they had a different attitude toward women, they were very brutal with them, in a word they were rapists, and they stole, and they carried knives. But the French had endured this for more than a hundred years and were willing to endure it for a hundred years more, in spite of the fact that Algeria was a great drain on the national pocketbook and the fact that any Algerian—due to the fact that Algeria was French, was, in fact, a French *département,* and was damn well going to stay that way—was free to come to Paris at any time and jeopardize the economy and prowl the streets and prey on French women. In short, the record of French generosity was so exemplary that it was impossible to believe that the children could seriously be bent on revolution.

Impossible for a Frenchman, perhaps, but not for me. I had watched the police, one sunny afternoon, beat an old, one-armed Arab peanut vendor senseless in the streets, and I had watched the unconcerned faces of the French on the café terraces, and the con-

Stalinists. The convulsion was the more ironical for me in that I had been an anti-Communist when America and Russia were allies. I had nearly been murdered on 14th Street, one evening, for putting down too loudly, in the presence of patriots, that memorable contribution to the War effort, the Warner Brothers production of *Mission To Moscow*. The very same patriots now wanted to burn the film and hang the filmmakers, and Warners, during the McCarthy era, went to no little trouble to explain their film away. Warners was abject, and so was nearly everybody else, it was a foul, ignoble time: and my contempt for most American intellectuals, and/or liberals dates from what I observed of their manhood then. I say most, not all, but the exceptions constitute a remarkable pantheon, even, or, rather, especially those who did not survive the flames into which their lives and their reputations were hurled. I had come home to a city in which nearly everyone was gracelessly scurrying for shelter, in which friends were throwing their friends to the wolves, and justifying their treachery by learned discourses (and tremendous tomes) on the treachery of the Comintern. Some of the things written during those years, justifying, for example, the execution of the Rosenbergs, or the crucifixion of Alger Hiss (and the beatification of Whittaker Chambers) taught me something about the irresponsibility and cowardice of the liberal community which I will never forget. Their performance, then, yet more than the combination of ignorance and arrogance with which this community has always protected itself against the deepest implications of black suffering, persuaded me that brilliance without passion is nothing more than sterility. It must be remembered, after all, that I did not begin meeting these people at the point that they began to meet *me:* I had been delivering their packages and emptying their garbage and taking their tips for years. (And they don't tip well.) And what I watched them do to each other during the McCarthy era was, in some ways, worse than anything they had ever done to me, for I, at least, had never been mad enough to depend on their devotion. It seemed very clear to me that they were lying about their motives and were being blackmailed by their guilt; were, in fact, at bottom, nothing more than the respectable issue of various immigrants, struggling to hold on to what they had acquired. For, intellectual activity, according to me, is, and must be, disinterested—the truth *is* a two-edged sword—and if one is not willing to be pierced by that sword, even to the extreme of dying on it, then all of one's intellectual activity is a masturbatory delusion and a wicked and dangerous fraud.

I made such motions as I could to understand what was happening, and to keep myself afloat. But I had been away too long. It was not only that I *could* not readjust myself to life in New York—it was also that I *would* not: I was never going to be anybody's nigger again. But I was now to discover that the world has more than one way of keeping you a nigger, has evolved more than one way of skinning the cat; if the hand slips here, it tightens there, and now I was off-ered, gracefully indeed: membership in the club. I had lunch at some elegant bistros, dinner at some exclu-sive clubs. I tried to be understanding about my coun-trymen's concern for difficult me, and unruly mine—and I really *was* trying to be understanding, though not without some bewilderment, and, eventually, some malice. I began to be profoundly uncomfortable. It was a strange kind of discomfort, a terrified appre-hension that I had lost my bearings. I did not al-together understand what I was hearing. I did not trust what I heard myself saying. In very little that I heard did I hear anything that reflected anything which *I* knew, or had endured, of life. My mother and my father, my brothers and my sisters were not pre-sent at the tables at which I sat down, and no one in the company had ever heard of them. My own begin-nings, or instincts, began to shift as nervously as the cigarette smoke that wavered around my head. I was not trying to hold on to my wretchedness. On the contrary, if my poverty was coming, at last, to an end, so much the better, and it wasn't happening a mo-ment too soon—and yet, I felt an increasing chill, as though the rest of my life would have to be lived in silence.

I think it may have been my own obsession with the McCarthy phenomenon which caused me to suspect cloaked with formulas that they no longer seemed to have any connection with it. They were all, for a while anyway, very proud of me, of course, proud that I had been able to crawl up to their level and been "accepted." What *I* might think of *their* level, how *I* might react to this "acceptance," or what this acceptance might cost me, were not among the questions which racked them in the midnight hour. One wondered, indeed, if anything could ever disturb their sleep. They walked the same streets I walked, after all, rode the same subways, must have seen the same increasingly desperate and hostile boys and girls, must, at least occasionally, have passed through the garment center. It is true that even those who taught at Columbia never saw Harlem, but, on the other hand, eveything that New York has become, in 1971, was visibly and swiftly beginning to happen in 1952: one had only to take a bus from the top of the city and ride through it to see how it was darkening and deteriorating, how human bewilderment and hostility rose, how human contact was endangered and dying. Of course, these liberals were not, as I was, forever being found by the police in the "wrong" neighborhood, and so could not have had first-hand knowledge of how gleefully a policeman translates his orders from above. But they had no right not to know that; if they did not know that, they knew nothing and had no right to speak as though they were responsible actors in their society; for their complicity with the patriots of that hour meant that the policeman was acting on *their* orders, too.

No, I couldn't hack it. When my first novel was finally sold, I picked up my advance and walked straight to the steamship office and booked passage back to France.

I place it here, though it occurred during a later visit: I found myself in a room one night, with my liberal friends, after a private showing of the French film, *The Wages of Fear*. The question on the floor was whether or not this film should be shown in the United States. The reason for the question was that the film contained unflattering references to American oil companies. I do not know if I said anything, or not; I rather doubt that I could have said much. I felt as paralyzed, fascinated, as a rabbit before a snake. I had, in fact, already seen the film in France. It had not occurred to me, or to anyone I knew, that the film was even remotely anti-American: by no stretch of the imagination could this be considered the film's *motif.* Yet, here were the autumn patriots, hotly discussing the dangers of a film which dared to suggest that American oil interests didn't give a shit about human life. There was a French woman in the room, tight-mouthed, bitter, far from young. She may or may not have been the widow of a Vichyite General, but her sympathies were in that region: and I will never forget her saying, looking straight at me, "We always knew that you, the Americans, would realize, one day, that you fought on the wrong side!"

I was ashamed of myself for being in that room: but, I must say, too, that I was glad, glad to have been a witness, glad to have come far enough to have heard the devil speak. That woman gave me something, I will never forget her, and I walked away from the welcome table.

Yet, hope—the hope that we, human beings, can be better than we are—dies hard; perhaps one can no longer live if one allows that hope to die. But it is also hard to see what one sees. One sees that most human beings are wretched, and, in one way or another, become wicked: because they are so wretched. And one's turning away, then, from what I have called the welcome table is dictated by some mysterious vow one scarcely knows one's taken—never to allow oneself to fall so low. Lower, perhaps, much lower, to the very dregs: but never there.

_____

When I came back to Paris at the end of the summer, most of the Arab cafés I knew had been closed. My favorite money-changer and low-life guide, a beautiful stone hustler, had disappeared, no one knew—or no one said—where. Another cat had had his eyes put out —some said by the police, some said by his brothers, because he was a police informer. In a sense, that beautiful, blinded boy who had been punished either as a traitor to France or as a traitor to Algeria, sums up the Paris climate in the years immediately preceding the revolution. One was either French, or Algerian; one could not be both.

There began, now, a time of rumor unlike anything I had ever been through before. In a way, I was somewhat insulated against what was happening to the Algerians, or was aware of it from a certain distance, because what was happening to the Algerians did not appear to be happening to the blacks. I was still operating, unconsciously, within the American framework, and, in that framework, since Arabs are paler than blacks, it is the blacks who would have suffered most. But the blacks, from Martinique and Senegal, and so on, were as visible and vivid as they had always been, and no one appeared to molest them or to pay them any particular attention at all. Not only was I operating within the American frame of reference, I was also a member of the American colony, and we were, in general, slow to pick up on what was going on around us.

Nevertheless, I began to realize that I could not find *any* of the Algerians I knew, not one; and since I could not find one, there was no way to ask about the others. They were in none of the dives we had frequented, they had apparently abandoned their rooms, their cafés, as I have said, were closed, and they were no longer to be seen on the Paris sidewalks, changing money, or selling their rugs, their peanuts, or themselves. We heard that they had been placed in camps around Paris, that they were being tortured there, that they were being murdered. No one wished to believe any of this, it made us exceedingly uncomfortable, and we felt that we should do something, but there was nothing we could do. We began to realize that there *had* to be some truth to these pale and cloudy rumors: one woman told me of seeing an Algerian hurled by the proprietor of a café in Pigalle *through* the café's *closed* plate-glass door. If she had not witnessed a murder, she had certainly witnessed a murder attempt. And, in fact, Algerians *were* being murdered in the streets, and corraled into prisons, and being dropped into the Seine, like flies.

Not only Algerians. Everyone in Paris, in those years, who was not, resoundingly, from the north of Europe was suspected of being Algerian; and the police were on every street corner, sometimes armed with machine guns. Turks, Greeks, Spaniards, Jews, Italians, American blacks, and Frenchmen from Marseilles, or Nice, were all under constant harassment, and we will never know how many people having not the remotest connection with Algeria were thrown into prison, or murdered, as it were, by accident. The son of a world-famous actor, and an actor himself, swarthy, and speaking no French—rendered speechless indeed by the fact that the policeman had a gun leveled at him—was saved only by the fact that he was close enough to his hotel to shout for the night porter, who came rushing out and identified him. Two young Italians, on holiday, did not fare so well: speeding merrily along on their Vespa, they failed to respond to a policeman's order to halt, whereupon the policeman fired, and the holiday came to a bloody end. Everyone one knew was full of stories like these, which eventually began to appear in the press, and one had to be careful how one moved about in the fabulous city of light.

I had never, thank God—and certainly not once I found myself living there—been even remotely romantic about Paris. I may have been romantic about London—because of Charles Dickens—but the romance lasted for exactly as long as it took me to carry my bags out of Victoria Station. My journey, or my flight, had not been *to* Paris, but simply *away* from America. For example, I had seriously considered going to work on a kibbutz in Israel, and I ended up in Paris almost literally by closing my eyes and putting my finger on a map. So I was not as demoralized by all of this as I would certainly have been if I had ever made the error of considering Paris the most civilized of cities and the French as the least primitive of peoples. I knew too much about the French Revolution for that. I had read too much Balzac for that. Whenever I crossed la place de la Concorde, I heard the tumbrils arriving, and the roar of the mob, and where the obelisk now towers, I saw—and see—*la guillotine.* Anyone who has ever been at the mercy of the people, then, knows something awful about us, will forever distrust

39

the popular patriotism, and avoids even the most con-
vivial of mobs.

Still, my flight had been dictated by my hope that I
could find myself in a place where I would be treated
more humanely than my society had treated me at
home, where my risks would be more personal, and
my fate less austerely sealed. And Paris had done this
for me: by leaving me completely alone. I lived in Paris
for a long time without making a single French friend,
and even longer before I saw the inside of a French
home. This did not really upset me, either, for Henry
James had been here before me and had had the
generosity to clue me in. Furthermore, for a black boy
who had grown up on Welfare and the chicken-shit
goodwill of American liberals, this total indifference
came as a great relief and, even, as a mark of respect.
If I could make it, I could make it; so much the better.
And if I couldn't, I couldn't—so much the worse. I
didn't want any help, and the French certainly didn't
give me any—they let me do it myself; and for that
reason, even knowing what I know, and unromantic as
I am, there will always be a kind of love story between
myself and that odd, unpredictable collection of bour-
geois chauvinists who call themselves *la France.*

Or, in other words, my reasons for coming to
France, and the comparative freedom of my life in
Paris, meant that my attitude toward France was very
different from that of any Algerian. He, and his broth-

—my life in Paris was to some extent protected by the fact that I carried a green passport. This passport proclaimed that I was a free citizen of a free country, and was not, therefore, to be treated as one of Europe's uncivilized, black possessions. This same passport, on the other side of the ocean, underwent a sea change and proclaimed that I was not an African prince, but a domestic nigger and that no foreign government would be offended if my corpse were to be found clogging up the sewers. I had never had occasion to reflect before on the brilliance of the white strategy: blacks didn't know each other, could barely speak to each other, and, therefore, could scarcely trust each other—and therefore, wherever we turned, we found ourselves in the white man's territory, and at the white man's mercy. Four hundred years in the West had certainly turned me into a Westerner—there was no way around that. But four hundred years in the West had also failed to bleach me—there was no way around *that*, either—and my history in the West had, for its daily effect, placed me in such mortal danger that I had fled, all the way around the corner, to France. And if I had fled, to Israel, a state created for the purpose of protecting Western interests, I would have been in yet a tighter bind: on which side of Jerusalem would I have decided to live? In 1948, no African nation, as such, existed, and could certainly neither have needed, nor welcomed, a penniless black American, with the possible exception of Liberia. But, even with black over-the battle of Algiers was really about was the fact that the French refused to give the Algerians the right to be wrong; refused to allow them, so to speak, that "existentialist" situation, of which the French, for a season, were so enamored; or, more accurately, did not even dare imagine that the Algerian situation could be "existentialist"; precisely because the French situation was so extreme. There was no way for him not to have known that Algeria was French only insofar as French power had decreed it to be French. It existed on the European map only insofar as European power had placed it there. It is power, not justice, which keeps rearranging the map, and the Algerians were not fighting the French for justice (of which, indeed, they must have had their fill by that time) but for the power to determine their own destinies.

It was during this time that Camus translated and directed, for the Mathurin Theatre, in Paris, William Faulkner's *Requiem for a Nun*, and an American magazine asked me to review it. I would almost certainly not have seen this production otherwise, for I had seen the play in New York, and I had read the book, and had found Faulkner's fable to be a preposterous bore. But I trotted off to the Mathurin Theatre to see it, taking along a gallant lady friend. And we suffered through this odd and interminable account of the sins of a white Southern lady, and her cardboard husband, and the nigger-whore-dope fiend maid, Nancy. Nancy, in order to arrest her mistress's headlong flight to self-

Neither of them could accurately, or usefully, be described as racists, in spite of Faulkner's declared intention of shooting Negroes in the streets if he found this necessary for the salvation of the state of Mississippi. This statement had to be read as an excess of patriotism, unlikely, in Faulkner's case, to lead to any further action. The mischief of the remark lay in the fact that it certainly encouraged others to such action. And Faulkner's portraits of Negroes, which lack a system of nuances that, perhaps, only a black writer can see in black life—for Faulkner could see Negroes only as they related to him, not as they related to each other—are nevertheless made vivid by the torment of their creator. He is seeking to exorcise a history which is also a curse. He wants the old order, which came into existence through unchecked greed and wanton murder, to redeem itself without further bloodshed—without, that is, any further menacing it-self—and without coercion. This, old orders never do, less because they would not than because they cannot. They cannot because they have always existed in rela-tion to a force which they have had to subdue. This subjugation is the key to their identity and the triumph and justification of their history, and it is also on this continued subjugation that their material well-being depends. One may see that the history, which is now indivisible from oneself, has been full of errors and excesses; but this is not the same thing as seeing that, for millions of people, this history—oneself—has been

Dakar. The "evolved," or civilized one is almost always someone educated by, and for, France, and some of "our" niggers, proving how well they have been educated, become spokesmen for "black" capitalism —a concept demanding yet more faith and infinitely more in schizophrenia than the concept of the Virgin Birth. Dakar is a French city on the West African coast, and a representative from Dakar is not necessarily a man from Senegal. He is much more likely to be a spiritual citizen of France, in which event he cannot possibly convey the actual needs of his part of Africa, or of Africa. And when such a dialogue truly erupts, it cannot avoid the root question of the possession of the land, and the exploitation of the land's resources. At that point, the cultural pretensions of history are revealed as nothing less than a mask for power, and thus it happens that, in order to be rid of Shell, Texaco, Coca-Cola, the Sixth Fleet, and the friendly American soldier whose mission it is to protect these investments, one finally throws Balzac and Shakespeare—and Faulkner and Camus—out with them. Later, of course, one may welcome them back, but on one's own terms, and, absolutely, on one's own land.

When the pagan and the slave spit on the cross and pick up the gun, it means that the halls of history are about to be invaded once again, destroying and dispersing the present occupants. These, then, can call only on their history to save them—that same history which, in the eyes of the subjugated, has already condemned them. Therefore, Faulkner hoped that American blacks would have the generosity to "go slow"— would allow white people, that is, the time to save themselves, as though they had not had more than enough time already, and as though their victims still believed in white miracles—and Camus repeated the word "justice" as though it were a magical incantation to which all of Africa would immediately respond. American blacks could not "go slow" because they had made a rendezvous with history for the purpose of taking their children out of history's hands. And Camus' "justice" was a concept forged and betrayed in Europe, in exactly the same way as the Christian church has betrayed and dishonored and blasphemed that Saviour in whose name they have slaughtered millions and millions and millions of people. And if this mighty objection seems trivial, it can only be because of the total hardening of the heart and the coarsening of the conscience among those people who believed that their power has given them the exclusive right to history. If the Christians do not believe in their Saviour (who has certainly, furthermore, failed to save them) why, then, wonder the unredeemed, should I abandon my gods for yours? For I *know* my gods are real: they have enabled me to withstand you.

In the fall of 1956, I was covering, for *Encounter* (or for the CIA) the first International Conference of Black Writers and Artists, at the Sorbonne, in Paris.

One bright afternoon, several of us, including the late Richard Wright, were meandering up the Boulevard St.-Germain, on the way to lunch. Much, if not most of the group was African, and all of us (though some only legally) were black. Facing us, on every newspaper kiosk on that wide, tree-shaded boulevard, were photographs of fifteen-year-old Dorothy Counts being reviled and spat upon by the mob as she was making her way to school in Charlotte, North Carolina. There was unutterable pride, tension, and anguish in that girl's face as she approached the halls of learning, with history, jeering, at her back.

It made me furious, it filled me with both hatred and pity, and it made me ashamed. Some one of us should have been there with her! I dawdled in Europe for nearly yet another year, held by my private life and my attempt to finish a novel, but it was on that bright afternoon that I knew I was leaving France. I could, simply, no longer sit around in Paris discussing the Algerian and the black American problem. Everybody else was paying their dues, and it was time I went home and paid mine.

———————

I took a boat home in the summer of 1957, intending to go South as soon as I could get the bread together. This meant, in my case, as soon as I could get an assignment. This was not so easy in 1957, and I was stuck in New York for a discouragingly long time. And now I had to begin to arrive at some kind of *modus vivendi* with New York—for here I was, home again, for the first time in nine years—to stay. *To stay:* if this thought chilled me, it also relieved me. It was only here, after all, that I would be able to find out what my journey had meant to me, or what it had made of me.

And I began to see New York in a different way, seeing beneath the formlessness, in the detail of a cornice, the shape of a window, the movement of stone steps—*stoep,* say the Dutch, and we say, *stoop*— beneath the nearly invincible and despairing noise, the sound of many tongues, all struggling for dominance. Since I was here to stay, I had to examine it, learn it all over again, and try to find out if I had ever loved it. But the question contained, or so I suspected, its own melancholy answer. If I had ever loved New York, that love had, literally, been beaten out of me; if I had ever loved it, my life could never have depended on so long an absence and so deep a divorce; or, if I had ever loved it, I would have been glad, not frightened, to be back in my home town. No, I didn't love it, at least not any more, but I was going to have to survive it. In order to survive it, I would have to watch it. And, though I had nightmares about that Southland which I had never seen, I was terribly anxious to get there, perhaps to corroborate the nightmare, but certainly to get out of what was once described to me as "the great unfinished city."

Finally, I got my assignment, and I went South. Something began, for me, tremendous. I met some of the noblest, most beautiful people a man can hope to meet, and I saw some beautiful and some terrible things. I was old enough to recognize how deep and strangling were my fears, how manifold and mighty my limits: but no one can demand more of life than that life do him the honor to demand that he learn to live with his fears, and learn to live, every day, both within his limits and beyond them.

I must add, for the benefit of my so innocent and criminal countrymen, that, today, fifteen years later, the photograph of Angela Davis has replaced the photograph of Dorothy Counts. These two photographs would appear to sum up the will of the Americans—heirs of all the ages—in relation to the blacks.

There comes floating up to me, out of a life I lived long ago—during the cybernetics craze, the Wilhelm Reich misapprehension, the Karen Horney precisions, that time, predating Sartre, when many of my friends vanished into the hills, or into anarchies called communes, or into orgone boxes, never to be seen, and certainly never to make love again—the memory of a young white man, beautiful, Jewish, American, who ate his wife's afterbirth, frying it in a frying pan. He did this because—who knows?—Wilhelm Reich, according to him, had ordered it. He comes floating up to me because, though he never knew it, I loved him, and the silence between us was the precise indication of how deeply something in me responded to, and is still bewildered by, his trouble. I remember his face when he told me about it, long after his courageous culinary effort. By this effort, he made his wife and child a part of himself. The question which has remained in my mind, no doubt, is why so extreme an effort should have been needed to prove a fact which should have been so obvious and so joyous. By the time he told me, he had lost both the wife and the child, was virtually adopting another one, black, this time, and, though he was younger than I, and I am speaking of a long time ago, had, emotionally, it seemed to me, ceased to exist. I got the impression that he had hurried himself through a late and tormented adolescence into an early middle age, with an almost audible sigh of relief, having encountered only theorems along the way: and, though he did not know it, was now helplessly and hopelessly in love with a small black boy, not more than ten. I do not mean to suggest that he had sexual designs on the boy. It might, indeed, have been better for him if he had, however outrageous that may sound —it would, at least, have landed him in deep emotional trouble and brought to the fore the question of his honor: I mean that he appeared to be able to love only the helpless. I have not seen this man in many years, and I hope that everything I say here has since been proven false. I hope, in short, that he has been able to live. But I have always been struck, in America, by an emotional poverty so bottomless, and a terror of human life, of human touch, so deep, that virtually no American appears able to achieve any viable, organic connection between his public stance and his private life. This is what makes them so baffling, so moving, so exasperating, and so untrustworthy. "Only connect," Henry James has said. Perhaps only an American writer would have been driven to say it, his very existence being so threatened by the failure, in most American lives, of the most elementary and crucial connections.

This failure of the private life has always had the most devastating effect on American public conduct, and on black-white relations. If Americans were not so terrified of their private selves, they would never have needed to invent and could never have become so dependent on what they still call "the Negro problem." This problem, which they invented in order to safeguard their purity, has made of them criminals and monsters, and it is destroying them; and this not from anything blacks may or may not be doing but because of the role a guilty and constricted white imagination has assigned to the blacks. That the scapegoat pays for the sins of others is well known, but this is only legend, and a revealing one at that. In fact, however the scapegoat may be made to suffer, his suffering cannot purify the sinner; it merely incriminates him the more, and it seals his damnation. The scapegoat, eventually, is released, to death: his murderer continues to live. The suffering of the scapegoat has resulted in seas of blood, and yet not one sinner has been saved, or changed, by this despairing ritual. Sin has merely been added to sin, and guilt piled upon guilt. In the private chambers of the soul, the guilty party is identified, and the accusing finger, there, is not legend, but consequence, not fantasy, but the truth. People pay for what they do, and, still more, for what they have allowed themselves to become. And they pay for it very simply: by the lives they lead. The crucial thing, here, is that the sum of these individual abdications menaces life all over the world. For, in the generality, as social and moral and political and sexual entities, white Americans are probably the sickest and certainly the most dangerous people, of any color, to be found in the world today. I may not have realized this before my first journey South. But, once I found myself there, I recognized that the South was a riddle which could be read only in the light, or the darkness, of the unbelievable disasters which had overtaken the private life.

I say, "riddle": not the riddle of what this unhappy people claim, madly enough, as their "folk" ways. I had been a nigger for a long time. I was not struck by their wickedness, for that wickedness was but the spirit and the history of America. What struck me was the unbelievable dimension of their sorrow. I felt as though I had wandered into hell. But, it must also be said that, if they were in hell, some among them were beginning to recognize what fuel, in themselves, fed the flames. Their sorrow placed them far beyond, exactly, as at that hour, it seemed to have placed them far beneath, their compatriots—who did not yet know that sorrow existed, and who imagined that hell was a condition to which others were sentenced. For this reason, and I am not the only black man who will say this, I have more faith in Southerners than I will ever have in Northerners: the mighty and pious North could never, after all, have acquired its wealth without utilizing, brutally, and consciously, those "folk" ways, and locking the South within them. And when this country's absolutely inescapable disaster levels it, it is in the South and not in the North that the rebirth will begin.

I went, first, if memory serves, to Charlotte, North Carolina, where I met, among others, *The Carolina Israelite.* I went to Little Rock, where I met, among others, Mr. and Mrs. Bates. I went to Atlanta, where I met, among others, Reverend Martin Luther King, Jr. I went to Birmingham. I went to Montgomery. I went to Tuskegee. I don't know how long I was on the road. The canvas suitcase I had carried down was so full of contraband by the time I lugged it, on one shoulder, up, that it burst in the middle of Grand Central Station, scattering underground secrets all over the floor: no one, luckily, exhibited the remotest curiosity. I managed to get it all together, tied the suitcase together with the belt from my trousers, and got up the stairs, into the city. I collapsed in the home of a friend who lived in what was not yet known as the East Village—when I had been a tenant, it was known as the Lower East Side—and, re-living my trip, surrendered to my nightmares, and, as far as the city was concerned, vanished. I could not take it on, I could not move out of that cold-water flat. I kept meaning to, I kept putting it off: for five days. I had called my sister, Gloria, from the station, so she knew that I was back in New York, but she did not know where. Therefore, my family and friends were searching for me in every Village street and bar and were considering the dubious and desperate extreme of calling the police. But, finally, I surfaced, fully conscious of how irresponsible I had been, and more than a little shaken by the realization that it had been a kind of retrospective terror which had paralyzed me so long. While in the South I had suppressed my terror well enough, in any case, to function; but when the pressure came off, a kind of wonder of terror overcame me, making me as useless as a snapped rubber band. This worried me exceedingly. I sensed in it a pattern which I was never, in fact, thoroughly to overcome. I will never forget the weary face of a black friend who had been searching for me for days, meeting me on Sixth Avenue as I was on my repentant way to the subway. He saw me as he turned from Waverly Place onto the avenue at the same time that I saw him. He stood stock-still as I was forced to walk toward him. A small, unwilling smile tugged at the corners of his lips. Then, I was in front of him and Lonnie said, "Well, *I'm* not going to curse you out. You've done it to yourself already." And he bought me a drink, and I went uptown to my sister's house, where I was sleeping on the couch in those days.

In the church, the preacher says, after an apparently meaningless anecdote, "I have said all that to say"—this: I doubt that I really knew much about terror before I went South. I do not mean, merely, though I very well might, that visceral reaction produced by the realization that one is facing one's own death. Then, as now, a Northern policeman, black or white, a white co-worker, or a black one, the colorless walls of precinct basements, the colorless handcuffs, the colorless future, are quite enough to introduce into one's life the stunning realization that that life can be ended at any moment. Furthermore, this terror can produce its own antidote: an overwhelming pride and rage, so that, whether or not one is ready to die, one gives every appearance of being willing to die. And at that moment, in fact, since retreat means accepting a death far worse, one *is* willing to die, hoping merely (God's last small mercy) to drag one's murderer along.

Not many among the redeemed have any sense of this passion, which they describe, without knowing how profoundly they are describing themselves, as suicidal. They mean that it is suicidal to contend with a force obviously, or apparently, greater than oneself and that they would never dream of doing such a thing. They also mean that they, by definition, by their numbers, are the greater force, and they never suspect to what merciless level of contempt this oblique and arrogant confession exposes them. A man who knows that he is facing death, or, more accurately, who knows that it is, after all, he, himself, who has insisted on and brought about this moment, may, involuntarily, helplessly, shout or weep, or even piss or shit in his pants, where he stands. But he will not turn back. To turn back is no longer among his possibilities: that is why he may shout or weep and his stink may then fill the air. He has brought himself to this moment, and this is *he*—if only for a moment—*he;* and the others are beneath him, and anonymous forever because they value their manhood less than he.

But the terror I am speaking of has little to do with one's specific fears for oneself: it relates to Dante's *I would not have believed that death had undone so many.*

I arrived in Little Rock, for example, during the famous—then famous, now all but forgotten—school convulsion. This convulsion, it is to be remembered, had apparently to do with the question of the integration or education of black children—integration and education are not synonyms, though Americans appear to think so. I am a city boy. My life began in the Big City, and had to be slugged out, toe to toe, on the city pavements. This meant that I was badly prepared for an entity like Little Rock, which, while it was certainly not yet a city, was, equally certainly, no longer a town. For that matter, it was not, geographically speaking, Southern. It was Southern only in truth, in terms of what its history had made of it, which is to say, ultimately, that it was Southern by choice. It was

Southern, therefore, to put it brutally, because of the history of America—the United States of America: and small black boys and girls were now paying for this holocaust. They were attempting to go to school. They were attempting to get an education, in a country in which education is a synonym for indoctrination, if you are white, and subjugation, if you are black. It was rather as though small Jewish boys and girls, in Hitler's Germany, insisted on getting a German education in order to overthrow the Third Reich. Here they were, nevertheless, scrubbed and shining, in their never-to-be-forgotten stiff little dresses, in their never-to-be-forgotten little blue suits, facing an army, facing a citizenry, facing white fathers, facing white mothers, facing the progeny of these co-citizens, facing the white past, to say nothing of the white present: small soldiers, armed with stiff, white dresses, and long or short dark blue pants, entering a leper colony, and young enough to believe that the colony could be healed, and saved. They paid a dreadful price, those children, for their missionary work among the heathen.

My terror involved my realization of the nature of the heathen. I did not meet any of my official murderers, not during that first journey. I met the Negro's friends. Thus, I was forced to recognize that, so long as your friend thinks of you as a Negro, you do not have a friend, and neither does he—your friend. You have become accomplices. Everything between you depends on what he cannot say to you, and what you will not say to him. And one of you is listening. If one of you is listening, to all those things, precisely, which are not being said, the intensity of this attention can scarcely be described as the attention one friend brings to another. If one of you is listening, both of you are plotting, though, perhaps, only one of you knows it. Both of you may be plotting to escape, but, since very different avenues appear to be open to each of you, you are plotting your escape from each other.

I have written elsewhere about those early days in the South, but from a distance more or less impersonal. I have never, for example, written about my unbelieving shock when I realized that I was being groped by one of the most powerful men in one of the states I visited. He had got himself sweating drunk in order to arrive at this despairing titillation. With his wet eyes staring up at my face, and his wet hands groping for my cock, we were both, abruptly, in history's ass-pocket. It was very frightening—not the gesture itself, but the abjectness of it, and the assumption of a swift and grim complicity: as my identity was defined by his power, so was my humanity to be placed at the service of his fantasies. If the lives of those children were in those wet, despairing hands, if their future was to be read in those wet, blind eyes, there was reason to tremble. This man, with a phone call, could prevent or provoke a lynching. This was one of the men you called (or had a friend call) in order to get your brother off the prison farm. A phone call from him might prevent your brother from being dug up, later, during some random archaeological expedition. Therefore, one had to be friendly: but the price for this was your cock.

This will sound an exaggerated statement to Americans, who will suppose it to refer, merely, to sexual (or sectional) abnormality. This supposition misses the point: which is double-edged. The slave knows, however his master may be deluded on this point, that he is called a slave because his manhood has been, or can be, or will be taken from him. To be a slave means that one's manhood is engaged in a dubious battle indeed, and this stony fact is not altered by whatever devotion some masters and some slaves may have arrived at in relation to each other. In the case of American slavery, the black man's right to his women, as well as to his children, was simply taken from him, and whatever bastards the white man begat on the bodies of black women took their condition from the condition of their mother: blacks were not the only stallions on the slave-breeding farms! And one of the many results of this loveless, money-making conspiracy was that, in giving the masters every conceivable sexual and commercial license, it also emasculated them of any human responsibility—to their women, to their children, to their wives, or to themselves. The results of this blasphemy resound in this country, on every private and public level, until this hour. When the man

Every black man walking in this country pays a tremendous price for walking: for men are not women, and a man's balance depends on the weight he carries between his legs. All men, however they may face or fail to face it, however they may handle, or be handled by it, know something about each other, which is simply that a man without balls is not a man; that the word *genesis* describes the male, involves the phallus, and refers to the seed which gives life. When one man can no longer honor this in another man—and this remains true even if that man is his lover—he has abdicated from a man's estate, and, hard upon the heels of that abdication, chaos arrives. It was something like this that I began to see, watching black men in the South and watching white men watching them. For that marvelously mocking, salty authority with which black men walked was dictated by the tacit and shared realization of the price each had paid to be able to walk at all. Their fights came out of that, their laughter came out of that, their curses, their tears, their decisions, their so menaced loves, their courage, and even their cowardice—and perhaps especially the stunning and unexpected changes they could play on these so related strings—their music, their dancing: it all came from the center. "No," said an elderly black man, standing in front of his barber shop, "I don't believe I'll join this voting registration drive. You see, I only cut the white folks' hair in here, and they'll close me up." He was very tall; as he said this, he seemed to be the fact that so many of the black men I talked to in the South in those years were—I can find no other word for them—heroic. I don't want to be misunderstood as having fallen into an easy chauvinism when I say that: but I don't see how any observer of the Southern scene in those years can have arrived at any other judgment. Their heroism was to be found less in large things than in small ones, less in public than in private. Some of the men I am thinking of could be very impressive publicly, too, and responsible for large events; but it was not this which impressed me. What impressed me was how they went about their daily tasks, in the teeth of the Southern terror. The first time I saw Reverend Shuttlesworth, for example, he came strolling across the parking lot of the motel where I was staying, his hat perched precariously between the back of his skull and the nape of his neck, alone. It was late at night, and Shuttlesworth was a marked man in Birmingham. He came up into my room, and, while we talked, he kept walking back and forth to the window. I finally realized that he was keeping an eye on his car—making sure that no one put a bomb in it, perhaps. As he said nothing about this, however, naturally I could not. But I was worried about his driving home alone, and, as he was leaving, I could not resist saying something to this effect. And he smiled—smiled as though I were a novice, with much to learn, which was true, and as though he would be glad to give me a few pointers, which, indeed, not much later on, he did—and told me he'd be all right and went downstairs and got into his car, switched on the motor and drove off into the soft Alabama night. There was no hint of defiance or bravado in his manner. Only, when I made my halting observation concerning his safety, a shade of sorrow crossed his face, deep, impatient, dark; then it was gone. It was the most impersonal anguish I had ever seen on a man's face. It was as though he were wrestling with the mighty fact that the danger in which he stood was as nothing compared to the spiritual horror which drove those who were trying to destroy him. They endangered him, but they doomed themselves.

I had never seen this horror, this poverty, before, though I had worked among Southerners, years before, when I was working for the Army, during the war. It was very frightening, disagreeable, and dangerous, but I was not, after all, in their territory—in a sense, or at least as they resentfully supposed, they were in mine. Also, I could, in a sense, protect myself against their depredations and the fear that they inspired in me by considering them, quite honestly, as mad. And I was too young for the idea of my death or destruction really to have taken hold of my mind. It is hard for anyone under twenty to realize that death has already assigned him a number, which is going to come up one day.

But I was not in my territory now. I was in territory absolutely hostile and exceedingly strange, and I was old enough to realize that I could be destroyed. It was lucky, oddly enough, that I had been out of the country for so long and had come South from Paris, in effect, instead of from New York. If I had not come from Paris, I would certainly have attempted to draw on my considerable kit of New York survival tricks, with what results I cannot imagine, for they would certainly not have worked in the South. But I had so far forgotten all my New York tricks as to have been unable to use them in New York, and now I was simply, helplessly, nakedly, an odd kind of foreigner and could only look on the scene that way. And this meant that, exactly like a foreigner, I was more fascinated than frightened.

There was more than enough to fascinate. In the Deep South—Florida, Georgia, Alabama, Mississippi, for example—there is the great, vast, brooding, welcoming and bloodstained land, beautiful enough to astonish and break the heart. The land seems nearly to weep beneath the burden of this civilization's unnameable excrescences. The people and the children wander blindly through their forest of billboards, antennae, Coca-Cola bottles, gas stations, drive-ins, motels, beer cans, music of a strident and invincible melancholy, stilted wooden porches, snapping fans, aggressively blue-jeaned buttocks, strutting crotches, pint bottles, condoms, in the weeds, rotting automobile corpses, brown as beetles, earrings flashing in the gloom of bus stops: over all there seems to hang a miasma of lust and longing and rage. Every Southern city seemed to me to have been but lately rescued from the swamps, which were patiently waiting to reclaim it. The people all seemed to remember their time under water, and to be both dreading and anticipating their return to that freedom from responsibility. Every black man, whatever his style, had been scarred, as in some tribal rite; and every white man, though white men, mostly, had no style, had been maimed. And, everywhere, the women, the most fearfully mistreated creatures of this region, with narrowed eyes and pursed lips—lips turned inward on a foul aftertaste— watched and rocked and waited. Some of them reminded me of a moment in my adolescent life when a church sister, not much older than I, who had been my girl friend, went mad, and was incarcerated. I went to visit her, in the women's wing of the asylum, and, coming out into the courtyard, stood there for a moment to catch my breath. Something, eventually, made me turn my head. Then I realized that I was standing in the sight of hundreds of incarcerated women. Behind those bars and windows, I don't know how many pairs of female eyes were riveted on the one male in that courtyard. I could dimly see their faces at the windows all up and down that wall; and they did not make a sound. For a moment I thought that I would never be able to persuade my feet to carry me away from that unspeakable, despairing, captive avidity.

My first night in Montgomery, I, like a good reporter, decided to investigate the town a little. I had been warned to be very careful how I moved about in the South after dark—indeed, I had been told not to move at all; but it was a pleasant evening, night just beginning to fall: suppertime. I walked a ways, past dark porches which were mostly silent, yet one felt a presence, or presences, sitting deep in the dark, sometimes silhouetted—but rarely—in the light from an open door, or one saw the ember of a cigarette, or heard a child's voice. It was very peaceful, and, though it may sound odd, I was very glad that I had come South. In spite of all that could have divided us, and in spite of the fact that some of them looked on me with an inevitable suspicion, I felt very much at home among the dark people who lived where I, if so much had not been disrupted, would logically have been born. I felt, beneath everything, a profound acceptance, an unfamiliar peace, almost as though, after despairing and debilitating journeys, I had, at last, come home. If there was, in this, some illusion, there was also some truth. In the years in Paris, I had never been homesick for anything American—neither waffles, ice cream, hot dogs, baseball, majorettes, movies, nor the Empire State Building, nor Coney Island, nor the Statue of Liberty, nor the *Daily News*, nor Times Square. All of these things had passed out of me as naturally and simply as taking a leak, and even less self-consciously. They might never have existed for me, and it made absolutely no difference to me if

I never saw them again. But I had missed my brothers and my sisters, and my mother—*they* made a difference. I wanted to be able to see them, and to see their children. I hoped that they wouldn't forget me. I missed Harlem Sunday mornings and fried chicken and biscuits, I missed the music, I missed the style—that style possessed by no other people in this world. I missed the way the dark face closes, the way dark eyes watch, and the way, when a dark face opens, a light seems to go on everywhere. I missed my brothers especially—missed David's grin and George's solemnity and Wilmer's rages, missed, in short, my connections, missed the life which had produced me and nourished me and paid for me. Now, though I was a stranger, I was home.

The racial dividing lines of Southern towns are baffling and treacherous for a stranger, for they are not as clearly marked as in the North—or not as clearly marked for *him*. I passed a porch with dark people; on the corner about a block away there was a restaurant. When I reached the corner, I entered the restaurant.

I will never forget it. I don't know if I can describe it. Everything abruptly froze into what, even at that moment, struck me as a kind of Marx Brothers parody of horror. Every white face turned to stone: the arrival of the messenger of death could not have had a more devastating effect than the appearance in the restaurant doorway of a small, unarmed, utterly astounded black man. I had realized my error as soon as I opened the door: but the absolute terror on all these white faces—I swear that not a soul moved—paralyzed me. They stared at me, I stared at them.

The spell was broken by one of those women, produced, I hope, only in the South, with a face like a rusty hatchet, and eyes like two rusty nails—nails left over from the Crucifixion. She rushed at me as though to club me down, and she barked—for it was not a human sound: "What you want, boy? What you want in here?" And then, a decontaminating gesture, "Right around there, boy. Right around there."

I had no idea what she was talking about. I backed out the door.

"Right around there, boy," said a voice behind me.

A white man had appeared out of nowhere, on the sidewalk which had been empty not more than a second before. I stared at him blankly. He watched me steadily, with a kind of suspended menace.

My first shock had subsided. I really had not had time to feel either fear or anger. Now, both began to rise in me. I knew I had to get off this street.

He had pointed to a door, and I knew immediately that he was pointing to the colored entrance.

And this was a dreadful moment—as brief as lightning, and far more illuminating. I realized that this man thought that he was being kind; and he was, indeed, being as kind as can be expected from a guide in hell. I realized that I must not speak to him, must not involve myself with him in any way whatever. I wasn't hungry anymore, but I certainly couldn't say *that*. Not only because this would have forced both of us to go further, into what confrontation I dared not think, but because of my Northern accent. It was the first time I realized that this accent was going to be a very definite liability; since I certainly couldn't change it, I was going to have to find some way of turning it into some kind of asset. But not at this very flaming moment, on this dark and empty street.

I saved my honor, hopefully, by reflecting, *Well, this is what you came here for. Hit it*—and I tore my eyes from his face and walked through the door he had so kindly pointed out.

I found myself in a small cubicle, with one electric light, and a counter, with, perhaps, four or five stools. On one side of the cubicle was a window. This window more closely resembled a cage-wire mesh, and an opening in the mesh. I was, now, in the back of the restaurant, though no one in the restaurant could see me. I was behind the restaurant counter, behind the hatchet-faced woman, who had her back to me, serving the white customers at the counter. I was nearly close enough to touch them, certainly close enough to touch her, close enough to kill them all, but they couldn't see me, either.

Hatchet-Face now turned to me, and said, "What you want?" This time, she did not say, "boy": it was no longer necessary.

I told her I wanted a hamburger and a cup of coffee,

which I didn't; but I wanted to see how those on my side of the mesh were served; and I wondered if she had to wash her hands each time, before she served the white folks again. Possibly not: for the hamburger came in paper, and the coffee in a paper cup.

I had all I could do to be silent as I paid her, and she turned away. I sat down on one of the stools, and a black man came in, grunted a greeting to me, went to the window, ordered, paid, sat down, and began to eat. I sat there for a while, thinking that I'd certainly asked for one hell of a gig. I wasn't sorry I'd come— I was never, in fact, ever to be sorry about that, and, until the day I die, I will always consider myself among the greatly privileged because, however inadequately, I was there. But I could see that the difficulties were not going to be where I had confidently placed them —in others—but in me. I was far from certain that I was equipped to get through a single day down here, and if I could not so equip myself then I would be a menace to all that others were trying to do, and a betrayal of their vast travail. They had been undergoing and overcoming for a very long time without me, after all, and they hadn't asked me to come: my role was to do a story and avoid becoming one. I watched the patient man as he ate, watched him with both wonder and respect. If he could do that, then the people on the other side of the mesh were right to be frightened—if he could do that, he could do anything and when he walked through the mesh there would be nothing to stop him. But *I* couldn't do it yet; my stomach was as tight as a black rubber ball. I took my hamburger and walked outside and dropped it into the weeds. The dark silence of the streets now frightened me a little, and I walked back to my hotel.

My hotel was a very funky black joint, so poverty stricken and for so long, that no one had anything to hide, or lose—not that they had stopped trying: they failed in the first endeavor as monotonously as they succeeded in the second. Life still held out the hope of what Americans, helplessly and honestly enough, call a "killing" and what blacks, revealingly enough, call a "hit." There seemed to be music all the time, someone was dancing all the time. It would have seemed, from a casual view, that this hotel was the gathering place for all the dregs of the town and that was true enough. But, since these dregs included the entire black society, it was a very various and revealing truth. Lodging for transient blacks, or entertainment for the locals, is a severely circumscribed matter in the Deep South, so that, for example, if one is not staying with friends or relatives, one stays in a hotel like mine, or, if one's friends or relatives decide to buy you a drink, they will bring you to the bar of this hotel. I liked it very much. I liked watching staid Baptist ministers and their plump, starched wives seated but a table away from the town's loose and fallen ladies and their unstarched men. I thought it healthy, because it reduced the possibilities of self-delusion—especially in those years. The Man had everybody in the same bag, and for the same reason, no matter what kind of suit he was wearing, or what kind of car he drove. And the people treated each other, it seemed to me, with rather more respect than was typical of New York, where, of course, the opportunities for self-delusion were, comparatively, so much greater.

Where whiskey was against the law, you simply bought your whiskey from the law enforcers. I did it, many times, all over the South, at first simply to find out if what I had been told was true—to see it with my own eyes and to pay the man with my own hands—and then, later, because life on the road began to run me ragged. It was almost impossible to get anything but bourbon, and the very smell of bourbon is still associated in my mind with the mean little eyes of deputy sheriffs and the holster on the hip and the ominous trees which line the highways. Nor can you get a meal anywhere in the South without being confronted with "grits"; a pale, lumpy, tasteless kind of porridge which the Southerner insists is a delicacy but which I believe they ingest as punishment for their sins. "What? you don't want no grits?" asks the wide-eyed waitress; not hostile yet, merely baffled. She moves away and spreads the word all over the region: "You see that man there? Well, he don't *eat* no grits"—and you are, suddenly, a marked man.

It is not difficult to become a marked man in the South—all you have to do, in fact, is go there. The booth I saw, not checking to see, and not caring whether I had entered the white or the black waiting room. I had resolved to avoid incidents, if possible, but it was already clear that it wouldn't always be possible. By the time I got my number, they watching me all the while, the MIA car drove up. And if the eyes of those men had had the power to pulverize that car, it would have been done, exactly as, in the Bible, the wicked city is leveled—I had never in all my life seen such a concentrated, malevolent poverty of spirit.

The Montgomery blacks were marching then, remember, and were in the process of bringing the bus company to its knees. What had begun in Montgomery was beginning to happen all over the South. The student sit-in movement has yet to begin. No one has yet heard of James Foreman or James Bevel. We have only begun to hear of Martin Luther King, Jr. Malcolm X has yet to be taken seriously. No one, except their parents, has ever heard of Huey Newton or Bobby Seale or Angela Davis. Emmett Till had been dead two years. Bobby Hutton and Jonathan Jackson have just mastered their first words, and, with someone holding them by the hand, are discovering how much fun it is to climb up and down the stairs. Oh, pioneers!—I got into the car, and we drove into town: the cradle of the Confederacy, the whitest town this side of Casablanca, and one of the most wretched on the face of the earth. And wretched because no one in authority in the town, the state, or the nation, had the force or the courage or the love to attempt to correct the manners or redeem the souls of those three desperate men, standing before that dismal airport, imagining that they were holding back a flood.

But how can I suggest any of the quality of some of those black men and women in the South then?—for it is important that I try. I can't name the names; sometimes because I can't remember them, or never knew them; and sometimes for other reasons. They were, the men, mostly preachers, or small tradesmen —this last word describes, or must be taken to suggest, a multitude of indescribable efforts—or professionals, such as teachers, or dentists, or lawyers. Because the South is, or certainly was then, so closed a community, their colors struck the light—the eye— far more vividly than these same colors strike one in the North: the prohibition, precisely, of the social mingling revealed the extent of the sexual amalgamation. Girls the color of honey, men nearly the color of chalk, hair like silk, hair like cotton, hair like wire, eyes blue, grey, green, hazel, black, like the gypsy's, brown like the Arab's, narrow nostrils, thin, wide lips, thin lips, every conceivable variation struck along incredible gamuts—it was not in the Southland that one could hope to keep a secret! And the niggers, of course, didn't try, though they knew their white brothers and sisters and papas, and watched them, daily, strutting around in their white skins. And sometimes shoveled garbage for their kith and kin, and sometimes went, hat in hand, looking for a job, or on more desperate errands. But: they could do it, knowing what they knew. And white men couldn't bear it—knowing that they knew: it is not only in the Orient that white is the color of death.

I remember the Reverend S., for example, a small, pale man, with hair resembling charred popcorn, and his tiny church, in a tiny town, where every black man was owned by a white man. In democratic parlance, of course, one says that every black man *worked* for a white man, and the democratic myth wishes us to believe that they worked together as men, and respected and honored and loved each other as men. But the democratic circumlocution pretends a level of liberty which does not exist and cannot exist until slavery in America comes to an end: in those towns, in those days, to speak only of the towns, and only of those days, a black man who displeased his employers was not going to eat for very long, which meant that neither he, nor his wife, nor children, were intended to live for very long. Yet, here he was, the Reverend S., every Sunday, in his pulpit, with his wife and children in the church, and bullet holes in the church basement, urging the people to move, to march, and to vote. For we believed, in those days, or made ourselves believe, that the black move to the registrar's office would be protected from Washington. I remember a Reverend D., who was also a grocer, and the night he described to me his conversion to nonviolence. A black grocer in the Deep South must also, like all grocers everywhere, purchase somewhere, somehow, the beans he places on his shelves to sell. This means that a black grocer who is one of the guiding spirits of a voting registration drive and who is also, virtually, a one-man car pool, can find remaining in business, to say nothing of his skin, an exceedingly strenuous matter. This was a big, cheerful man, as strong as an ox and stubborn as a mule, a fly not destined for the fly-paper, and he stayed in business. It cost him something. Bombing was not yet the great Southern sport which it was to become: they simply hurled bricks through his windows. He armed himself and his sons and they sat in the dark store night after night, waiting for their co-citizens—who, knowing they were armed, did not appear. And then, one morning, after the long night, the Reverend D. decided that this was no way for a man or a woman or a child to live. He may, of course, by this time, have been forced to change his mind again, but he was the first person to make the concept of nonviolence real to me: for it entered, then, precisely, the realm of individual and, above all, private choice and I saw, for the first time, how difficult a choice it could be.

to be baptized

All of the Western nations have been caught in a lie, the lie of their pretended humanism; this means that their history has no moral justification, and that the West has no moral authority. Malcolm, yet more concretely than Frantz Fanon—since Malcolm operated in the Afro-American idiom, and referred to the Afro-American situation—made the nature of this lie, and its implications, relevant and articulate to the people whom he served. He made increasingly articulate the ways in which this lie, given the history and the power of the Western nations, had become a global problem, menacing the lives of millions. "Vile as I am," states one of the characters in Dostoevski's *The Idiot*, "I don't believe in the wagons that bring bread to humanity. For the wagons that bring bread to humanity, without any moral basis for conduct, may coldly exclude a considerable part of humanity from enjoying what is brought; so it has been already." Indeed. And so it is now. Dostoevski's personage was speaking of the impending proliferation of railways, and the then prevalent optimism (which was perfectly natural) as to the uplifting effect this conquest of distance would have on the life of man. But Dostoevski saw that the rise of this power would "coldly exclude a considerable part of humanity." Indeed, it was on this exclusion that the rise of this power inexorably depended; and now the excluded—"so it has been already"—whose lands have been robbed of the minerals, for example, which go into the building of railways and telegraph wires and TV sets and jet airliners and guns and bombs and fleets, must attempt, at exorbitant cost, to buy their manufactured resources back—which is not even remotely possible, since they must attempt this purchase with money borrowed from their exploiters. If they attempt to work out their salvation—their autonomy—on terms dictated by those who have excluded them, they are in a delicate and dangerous position, and if they refuse, they are in a desperate one: it is hard to know which case is worse. In both cases, they are confronted with the relentless necessities of human life, and the rigors of human nature. Anyone, for example, who has worked in, or witnessed, any of the "anti-poverty" programs in the American ghetto has an instant understanding of "foreign aid" in the "underdeveloped" nations. In both locales, the most skillful adventurers improve their material lot; the most dedicated of the natives are driven mad or inactive—or underground—by frustration; while the misery of the hapless, voiceless millions is increased—and not only that: their reaction to their misery is described to the world as criminal. Nowhere is this grisly pattern clearer than it is in America today, but what America is doing within her borders, she is doing around the world. One has only to remember that American investments cannot be considered safe wherever the population cannot be considered tractable; with this in mind, consider the American reaction to the Jew who boasts of sending arms to Israel, and the probable fate of an American black who wishes to stage a rally for the purpose of sending arms to black South Africa.

America proves, certainly, if any nation ever has, that man cannot live by bread alone; on the other hand, men can scarcely begin to react to this principle until they—and, still more, their children—have enough bread to eat. Hunger has no principles, it simply makes men, at worst, wretched, and, at best, dangerous. Also, it must be remembered—it cannot be overstated—that those centuries of oppression are also the history of a system of thought, so that both the ex-man who considers himself master and the ex-man who is treated like a mule suffer from a particular species of schizophrenia, in which each contains the other, in which each longs to be the other: "What connects a slave to his master," observes David Caute, in his novel, *The Decline of the West*, "is more tragic than that which separates them."

It is true that political freedom is a matter of power and has nothing to do with morality; and if one had ever hoped to find a way around this principle, the performance of power at bay, which is the situation of the Western nations, and the very definition of the American crisis, has dashed this hope to pieces. Moreover, as habits of thought reinforce and sustain the habits of power, it is not even remotely possible for the excluded to become included, for this inclusion means, precisely, the end of the *status quo*—or would result, as so many of the wise and honored would put it, in a mongrelization of the races.

But for power truly to feel itself menaced, it must somehow sense itself in the presence of another power —or, more accurately, an energy—which it has not known how to define and therefore does not really know how to control. For a very long time, for example, America prospered—or seemed to prosper: this prosperity cost millions of people their lives. Now, not even the people who are the most spectacular recipients of the benefits of this prosperity are able to endure these benefits: they can neither understand them nor do without them, nor can they go beyond them. Above all, they cannot, or dare not, assess or imagine the price paid by their victims, or subjects, for this way of life, and so they cannot afford to know why the victims are revolting. They are forced, then, to the conclusion that the victims—the barbarians—are revolting against all established civilized values—which is both true and not true—and, in order to preserve these values, however stifling and joyless these values have caused their lives to be, the bulk of the people desperately seek out representatives who are prepared to make up in cruelty what both they and the people lack in conviction.

This is a formula for a nation's or a kingdom's decline, for no kingdom can maintain itself by force alone. Force does not work the way its advocates seem to think it does. It does not, for example, reveal to the victim the strength of his adversary. On the contrary, it reveals the weakness, even the panic of his adversary, and this revelation invests the victim with patience. Furthermore, it is ultimately fatal to create too many victims. The victor can do nothing with these victims, for they do not belong to him, but—to the victims. They belong to the people he is fighting. The people know this, and as inexorably as the roll call— the honor roll—of victims expands, so does their will become inexorable: they resolve that these dead, their brethren, shall not have died in vain. When this point is reached, however long the battle may go on, the victor can never be the victor: on the contrary, all his energies, his entire life, are bound up in a terror he cannot articulate, a mystery he cannot read, a battle he cannot win—he has simply become the prisoner of the people he thought to cow, chain, or murder into submission.

Power, then, which can have no morality in itself, is yet dependent on human energy, on the wills and desires of human beings. When power translates itself into tyranny, it means that the principles on which that power depended, and which were its justification, are bankrupt. When this happens, and it is happening now, power can only be defended by thugs and mediocrities—and seas of blood. The representatives of the *status quo* are sickened and divided, and dread looking into the eyes of their young; while the excluded begin to realize, having endured everything, that they *can* endure everything. They do not know the precise shape of the future, but they know that the future belongs to them. They realize this—paradoxically—by the failure of the moral energy of their oppressors and begin, almost instinctively, to forge a new morality, to create the principles on which a new world will be built.

My sister, Paula, and my brother, David, and I lived together in London for a while in 1968. London was very peaceful, partly because we hardly ever went out. The house was big, so that we were not on top of each other, and all of us could cook. Besides, going out was hazardous. London was reacting to its accelerating racial problem and compounding the disaster by denying that it had one. My famous face created a certain kind of hazard—or hazards: for example, I remember a girl sitting next to me in a cinema suddenly *seeing* me in the light from the match with which she was lighting her cigarette. She stared and shook—I could not tell whether she was about to cry *Rape!* or ask for an autograph. In the event, she moved away. My dusky tribe had the same troubles, without the tremendous pause.

Nevertheless, London was still far from being as hysterical and dangerous as New York. Eventually, of course, black Englishmen, Indians, students, conscientious objectors, and CIA infiltrators—no doubt— tracked me down, as we had known was inevitable. Dick Gregory came to town and we shared a platform before part of London's black community. A British columnist told his readers before or during this time that he wished I would either "drop dead or shut up"; and on King's Road, near our house, British hippies paraded one day, carrying banners, one of which read, "Keep Britain Black." I felt myself in London on borrowed time, for sometime before, the Home Office, as I learned when I landed at Heathrow Airport, had declared me *persona non grata* in Britain. They had let me land, finally, but it took awhile. (They had thrown Stokely out about a week before.) I thought of the late Lorraine Hansberry's statement (to me) concerning the solidarity of the Western powers, and the impossibility, for such as we, of hoping for political asylum anywhere in the West. I thought of Robert Williams, who had not intended and almost surely never desired, to go East. And I thought of Malcolm.

Alex Haley wrote *The Autobiography of Malcolm X*. Months before the foregoing, in New York, he and Elia Kazan and I had agreed to do it as a play—and I still wish we had. We were vaguely aware that Hollywood was nibbling for a book, but, as Hollywood is always nibbling, it occurred to no one, certainly not to me, to take these nibbles seriously. It simply was not a subject which Hollywood could manage, and I didn't see any point in talking to them about it. But the book was sold to an independent producer, named Marvin Worth, who would produce it for Columbia Pictures. By this time, I was already in London; and I was also on the spot. For, while I didn't believe Hollywood could do it, I didn't quite see, since they declared themselves sincerely and seriously willing to attempt it, how I could duck the challenge. What it came to, in fact, was an enormous question: to what extent was I prepared again to gamble on the good faith of my countrymen?

In that time, now so incredibly far behind us, when the Black Muslims meant to the American people exactly what the Black Panthers mean today, and when they were described in exactly the same terms by that High Priest, J. Edgar Hoover, and when many of us believed or made ourselves believe that the American state still contained within itself the power of self-confrontation, the power to change itself in the direction of honor and knowledge and freedom, or, as Malcolm put it, "to atone," I first met Malcolm X. Perhaps it says a great deal about the black American experience, both negatively and positively, that so many should have believed so hard, so long, and paid such a price for believing: but what this betrayed belief says about white Americans is very accurately and abjectly summed up by the present, so-called Nixon Administration.

I had heard a great deal about Malcolm, as had everyone else, and I was a little afraid of him, as was everyone else, and I was further handicapped by having been out of the country for so long. When I returned to America, I again went South, and thus, imperceptibly, found myself mainly on the road. I saw Malcolm before I met him. I had just returned from someplace like Savannah, I was giving a lecture somewhere in New York, and Malcolm was sitting in the first or second row of the hall, bending forward at such an angle that his long arms nearly caressed the ankles of his long legs, staring up at me. I very nearly panicked. I knew Malcolm only by legend, and this legend, since I was a Harlem street boy, I was sufficiently astute to distrust. I distrusted the legend because we, in Harlem, have been betrayed so often. Malcolm might be the torch white people claimed he was—though, in general, white America's evaluations of these matters would be laughable and even pathetic did not these evaluations have such wicked results—or he might be the hustler I remembered from my pavements. On the other hand, Malcolm had no reason to trust me, either—and so I stumbled through my lecture, with Malcolm never taking his eyes from my face.

It must be remembered that in those great days I was considered to be an "integrationist"—this was never, quite, my own idea of myself—and Malcolm was considered to be a "racist in reverse." This formulation, in terms of power—and power is the arena in which racism is acted out—means absolutely nothing: it may even be described as a cowardly formulation. The powerless, by definition, can never be "racists," for they can never make the world pay for what they feel or fear except by the suicidal endeavor which makes them fanatics or revolutionaries, or both; whereas, those in power can be urbane and charming and invite you to those which they know you will never own. The powerless must do their own dirty work. The powerful have it done for them.

Anyway: somewhat later, I was the host, or moderator, for a radio program starring Malcolm X and a sit-in student from the Deep South. I was the moderator because both the radio station and I were afraid that Malcolm would simply eat the boy alive. I didn't want to be there, but there was no way out of it. I had come prepared to throw various camp stools under the child, should he seem wobbly; to throw out the life-line whenever Malcolm should seem to be carrying the child beyond his depth. Never has a moderator been less needed. Malcolm understood that child and talked to him as though he were talking to a younger brother, and with that same watchful attention. What most struck me was that he was not at all trying to proselytize the child: he was trying to make him think. He was trying to do for the child what he supposed, for too long a time, that the Honorable Elijah had done for him. But I did not think of that until much later. I will never forget Malcolm and that child facing each other, and Malcolm's extraordinary gentleness. And that's the truth about Malcolm: he was one of the gentlest people I have ever met. And I am sure that the child remembers him that way. That boy, by the way, was vehemently non-stop and Malcolm was young and looked younger; this caused his opponents to suppose that Malcolm was reckless. Nothing could have been less reckless, more calculated, even to those loopholes he so often left dangling. These were not loopholes at all, but hangman's knots, as whoever rushed for the loophole immediately discovered. Whenever this happened, the strangling interlocutor invariably looked to me, as being the more "reasonable," to say something which would loosen the knot. Mr. Schuyler often *did* say something, but it was always the wrong thing, giving Malcolm yet another opportunity. All I could do was elaborate on some of Malcolm's points, or modify, or emphasize, or seem to try to clarify, but there was no way I could disagree with him. The others were discussing the past or the future, or a country which may once have existed, or one which may yet be brought into existence—Malcolm was speaking of the bitter and unanswerable present. And it was too important that this be heard for anyone to attempt to soften it. It was important, of course, for white people to hear it, if they were still able to hear; but it was of the utmost importance for black people to hear it, for the sake of their morale. It was important for them to know that there was someone like them, in public life, telling the truth about their condition. Malcolm considered himself to be the spiritual property of the people who produced him. He did not consider himself to be their saviour, he was far too modest for that, and

ine revolutionary, a virile impulse long since fled from
the American way of life—in himself, indeed, he was
a kind of revolution, both in the sense of a return to
a former principle, and in the sense of an upheaval. It
is pointless to speculate on his probable fate had he
been legally white. Given the white man's options, it
is probably just as well for all of us that he was legally
black. In some church someday, so far unimagined
and unimaginable, he will be hailed as a saint. Of
course, this day waits on the workings of the temporal
power which Malcolm understood, at last, so well.
Rome, for example, has just desanctified some saints
and invented, if one dares to use so utilitarian a word
in relation to so divine an activity, others, and the
Pope has been to Africa, driven there, no doubt, however belatedly, by his concern for the souls of black
folk: who dares imagine the future of such a litany as
black like me! Malcolm, anyway, had this much in common with all real saints and prophets, he had the
power, if not to drive the money-changers from the
temple, to tell the world what they were doing there.

For reasons I will never understand, on the day that
I realized that a play based on *The Autobiography* was
not going to be done, that sooner or later I would have
to say yes or no to the idea of doing a movie, I flew to
Geneva. I will never know why I flew to Geneva, which
is far from being my favorite town. I will never know
how it is that I arrived there with no toilet articles
whatever, no toothbrush, no toothpaste, no razor, no

hairbrush, no comb, and virtually no clothes. Furthermore, I have a brother-in-law and a sister-in-law living in Geneva of whom I'm very fond and it didn't even occur to me that they were there. All that I seem to have brought with me is *The Autobiography*. And I sat in the hotel bedroom all the weekend long, with the blinds drawn, reading and re-reading—or, rather, endlessly traversing—the great jungle of Malcolm's book.

The problems involved in a cinematic translation were clearly going to be formidable, and wisdom very strongly urged that I have nothing to do with it. It could not possibly bring me anything but grief. I still would have much preferred to have done it as a play, but that possibility was gone. I had grave doubts and fears about Hollywood. I had been there before, and I had not liked it. The idea of Hollywood doing a truthful job on Malcolm could not but seem preposterous. And yet—I didn't want to spend the rest of my life thinking: *It could have been done if you hadn't been chicken.* I felt that Malcolm would never have forgiven me for that. He had trusted me in life and I believed he trusted me in death, and that trust, as far as I was concerned, was my obligation.

From Geneva, I eventually went to London, to join my brother and sister. It was from London that I wired Kazan to say that the play was off, and I was doing the movie. This was only to take K. off the hook, for I wired no one else, had made no agreement to do the movie, and was very troubled and uncertain in my own mind.

———————————

Sometime during all this, through William Styron, I learned that a friend of mine, black, was in prison in Hamburg, Germany, charged with murder. This was William A. (Tony) Maynard, Jr., who had worked for me for some time, several years before, as bodyguard and chauffeur and man Friday. He had been arrested by Interpol and was being held in a Hamburg prison, from which he would probably be extradited to the States. The murder had been committed in New York's Greenwich Village in April of 1967. Tony knew Bill Styron because he had often driven me to Bill's house in Connecticut, and his letter to Bill, since he knew Bill to be rather more stationary than I, was a way of alerting me, and any other friends he had outside, of his desperate situation.

I did not doubt his innocence. Tony is a big man and can be very loud, is far from discreet, and has done his share of street fighting: but it is hard to imagine him killing anybody, especially, as was claimed, with a sawed-off shotgun. No one who knows Tony can believe that he would ever so lower himself as to be seen with so inelegant a weapon. For he has, in fact, a kind of pantherlike, street-boy elegance—he walks something like a cat—and a tricky, touchy, dangerous pride, which, in the years we worked together, kept him in all kinds of fruitless trouble; and he had a taste for white women (who had a taste for him) which made him, especially given his aggressively virile good looks, particularly unattractive to the NYPD. I had not seen Tony in some years. We had worked together in civil rights demonstrations and rallies, but, after the bombing of the Birmingham Sunday school—a much underrated event in this country's shameful history, and one which had a devastating effect on all black people—we had had a serious disagreement concerning the strategy needed to handle a rent strike, and had, thereafter, gone our separate ways. But I still considered him a friend. I wrote to him and I flew from London to Hamburg to visit him.

That winter, the beginning of 1968, London was cold, but damp and grey. Hamburg was frosty and dry as a bone, and blinding with ice and snow; and the sun, which never came to London, loitered in Hamburg all day long: *über alles*. Germans say that Hamburg is the German city which most resembles London. It is hard to know, from their tone, whether they are bragging or complaining, and it did not really remind me of London, lacking London's impressive sprawl; yet, it did confirm my ancient sense of the British and the Germans as cousins. Hamburg looks like a city built only for the purposes of affairs of state—an extraordinary sequence of stony façades. It makes one think of trumpets; there should be at least six trumpeters on every roof. The people are as friendly as people are in

London, and in the same way: with a courtesy as final as the raised drawbridge and as unsettling as the deep moat at one's feet. Behind the façade, of course, lives the city, furtive, paranoiac, puritanical, obsessed and in love with what it imagines to be sin—and also with what it imagines to be joy, it being difficult in Western culture to distinguish between these two. The prison was not far from my hotel, and I eventually acquired enough of a sense of direction to be able to walk from one castle to another. All the time I spent in Hamburg was spent between these two fixed points. The hotel was called The Four Seasons; because of the Maynard case, I once called Senator Javits from there; and ran into Pierre Salinger in the lobby once, he on his way out, I on my way in. If he had not been rushing out and if I had known him better, I might have tried to discuss the case with him. I needed help and advice and I have always rather liked Mr. Salinger. But I am not very good at buttonholing people, and besides I have learned that it frightens them.

It is not an easy matter to be allowed to visit a prisoner. Without the really extraordinary cooperation of my German publishers, I could never have managed it at all. But manage it we did, and so the day came when I was deposited in the waiting room of the prison at Holstenglacis.

The prison is part of a complex of intimidating structures, scattered over quite a large area—a little like the complex on l'Ile de la Cité in Paris, or the complex on Center Street in New York—but it resembles neither of them. It is more medieval than either, and gives the impression of being far more isolated—though, as I say, I could walk to it from my exceedingly fashionable hotel. Yet, the streets were torn up all around it—men at work; I learned to walk from there because taxis seemed never to come anywhere near it; there was a tramline, but I did not know how to use it, and it also seemed to skirt the prison. The only people I ever saw around there were clearly connected with the prison, or were visitors; you could tell the lawyers by their briefcases and their slightly chastened air of self-importance. To visit the prisoner, one had, of course, to have a pass. I am not, legally, related to Tony by blood, and my only pretext to have the right to visit (a right later to be taken from me) was that I was the only friend he had in Germany, and I had traveled quite a long way to see him. This was all arranged between my publishers and the lawyer, and I will never quite know how it was done. But the lawyer rang the bell, anyway, one frosty afternoon, before the great door, which opened and let us in. Then, I was deposited in the waiting room, and before me, at the height of two or three steps, was the great barred door which led to the interior of the prison. There were two or three people in the room with me. One man silently offered me a cigarette and, silently, I took it. The smoke between us, then, was all that we could manage of communion.

I was frightened in a way very hard to describe. The fact that this was the fabled Germany of the Third Reich, and this was a German prison, certainly had something to do with it. I was not so much afraid to see him as I was afraid of what might have happened to him—in him—the way one feels when about to see a loved one who has encountered great misfortune. One does not know what is left of the person. Human help often arrives too late, and if the person has really turned his face to the wall, no human being can help. The great barred door had opened often, letting people in or out; then, I was called or beckoned, and mounted the stone steps, standing before the bars; the turnkey smiled at me as he turned the key in the lock. Then I was led into another waiting room, narrow, two long benches on either side of a long table. The prisoners sat on one side, their visitors on the other. The guard stood at the door. Tall, and thinner than I had ever seen him, his high cheekbones pushing out of his skin, his hair too long, wearing clothes he hated, and with his eyes both wet and blazing, Tony stood and smiled. We held each other a moment, and sat down, facing each other, and Tony grinned: I saw that he hadn't turned his face to the wall.

"Hey—!" he said, "how you doing?"

The room was very crowded, and I hardly knew what to say. It would be hard to discuss his case.

"Upon my soul," said Tony, "I didn't do it."

I was glad he said it, though he didn't have to say it.

"Upon my soul," I said, "we'll get you out."

Between the night and the morning of April 3–4, in 1967, a Marine, Michael E. Kroll, was murdered on West 3rd Street, in Greenwich Village. He was killed, according to the newspaper stories, as a result of his intervention in a heated argument which a young sailor, Michael Crist, was having with two men, one white and one black. The black man is described as being about five feet, eight inches, and about twenty years old. (Tony was then twenty-seven, and is over six feet tall.) The two men, the black and the white, then walked away, but Kroll and the sailor apparently followed them and another argument ensued, which ended when the black man produced a sawed-off shotgun from beneath his jacket and shot the Marine in the head, killing him instantly. Then, the two men ran away. The claim was that all this happened because the black man had made an indecent proposal to the sailor.

"Can you see me doing that?" Tony asked. His face was extraordinarily vivid with the scorn he felt for so much of the human race. "Since when have I even *talked*"—his face convulsed as though he were vomiting—"to punks like that?"

And, truly, anyone knowing Tony, and hearing such

a description of his conduct, would have been forced to the conclusion that Tony had suddenly gone mad. Tony barely spoke when spoken to by strangers— when we worked together, it was his unending complaint that I was "too nice to these mothers"; he treated nearly everyone not within his immediate entourage with a bored, patient contempt. It was impossible to imagine the arrogant Tony walking through Village streets accosting strangers. As for the indecent proposal, the only way *that* could be explained was for the sailor to have mistaken a curse for an invitation. But it was difficult to imagine Tony speaking to him at all, and also hard to imagine that the sailor would have accosted him. Tony looks dangerous. And Tony could not have engaged in such conduct even if he were drunk, for the very good reason that he could not *get* drunk—long before he got drunk, he got sick. In short, in order to believe any of this, it would be necessary to invent a Tony whom no one knew.

But that, of course, would pose no difficulty for the police or the jury or the judge.

"Before I left New York"—this is another black friend of mine speaking to me, in Paris, many years ago—"well, you know, I was living with this white chick and we went around together, naturally, and we used to have coffee late at night, or early in the morning in this joint on Sheridan Square. And the neighborhood people didn't like it, and the cops didn't like

it says about them. When we walked out in the evening, then, she would leave ahead of me, alone. I
would give her about five minutes, and then I would
walk out alone, taking another route, and meet her on
the subway platform. We would not acknowledge each
other. We would get into the same subway car, sitting
at opposite ends of it, and walk, separately, through
the streets of the free and the brave, to wherever we
were going—a friend's house, or the movies. There
was only one restaurant, eventually, in which we ever
ate together, and it was run by a black woman. We
were fighting for our lives, and we were very young.
As for the police, our protectors, we would never have
dreamed of calling one. Our connection caused us to
be menaced by the police in ways indescribable and
nearly inconceivable; and the police egged on the
populace, stood laughing and talking while we were
spit on, and cursed. When with a girl, I never ran, I
couldn't: except once, when a girl I had been sleeping
with slapped me in the face in the middle of Washington Square Park. She was pulling rank, she was crying
Rape!—and then I ran. I still remember the day and
the hour, and the sunlight, the faces of the people, and
the girl's face—she had short red hair—and I will
never forgive that girl. I am astonished until today that
I have both my eyes and most of my teeth and func-
tioning kidneys and my sexual equipment: but small
black boys have the advantage of being able to curl
themselves into knots, and roll with the kicks and the

punches. Of course, I was a target for the police. I was black and visible and helpless and the word was out to "get" me, and so, soon, I, too, hauled ass. And the prisons of this country are full of boys like the boy I was.

"All right," cried Tony, with tears in his eyes, "I'm twenty-eight, and I'm a criminal, right? I've got a record—now they can do anything they want!"

Tony had been arrested about four years earlier, as a civil rights demonstrator—that stays on the books; then on a narcotics charge; then charged with stealing an overcoat—"I was running a business—who's going to steal an overcoat out of his own shop!"—and then charged with stealing a car. He was prosecuted only on the car-theft charge, which has since been dropped. Nevertheless, the car-theft charge marked the most important turning point of his life. He was held for something like two months—this was after the murder, and long before he was connected with it—and then released on bail. But a thoroughly shaken Tony, having been assured by the police that they would "get" him, jumped bail and went to Germany. He had been there before and had been happy there. His flight turned out to be his greatest error: but he could not have supposed that he would be arrested in Germany for having been accused of stealing a car—particularly as Tony's brand of arrogance causes him to act as if his private knowledge of his innocence constitutes irrefutable public proof. With his lofty *I would never do a thing like that*, he dismisses the accusation and is affronted—and surprised—when others do not take him at what he supposes to be his sacred word. And, in fact, almost the very first thing he did in Germany was to register his presence with the American Embassy and give them his address—unlikely conduct indeed for anyone supposing himself to be suspected of murder.

The murder occurred in April. The alleged car theft took place before the murder, but Tony was indicted on the car-theft charge well after the murder occurred, sometime in May. He was in jail for about two months and then released on bail. He arrived in Hamburg on October 22. On October 25, a Detective Hanst, in New York, swore out a complaint which declared that "as a result of information received and investigation made," Maynard was guilty of homicide. On October 27, a Judge Weaver, in New York, cabled the Hamburg chief of police demanding Maynard's arrest. It is not until October 31 that the deposition on which the entire case rests makes its appearance. This is signed by a certain Dennis Morris, whose address is in Brooklyn, and he identifies Tony Maynard by means of a passport-size snapshot. His deposition reads: "That on the morning of April 3, 1967 [but the crime is alleged to have taken place on the morning of the fourth] I was on West 4th Street, near Sixth Avenue, in the city, county, and state of New York, and saw a man, now known to me as Wm. A. Maynard, Jr., whose photograph on which I have placed my initials appears below and is part hereof, shoot and kill a man now known to me as Michael E. Kroll. I then saw said Wm. A. Maynard, Jr. run away from the scene of the crime."

This document, to say nothing of the date of its appearance, strikes me as extraordinary. It appears six days after Hanst's warrant and four days after Judge Weaver's cable—to say nothing of the fact that this authoritative identification of the murderer, by means of a photograph, occurs seven months after the event. Dennis Morris has made no appearance until this moment, and no one knows anything about him. The logical eyewitness, Crist, who was locked in an eyeball to eyeball confrontation with the murderer, has entirely disappeared. (He is to reappear during Tony's trial, armed with a most engaging reason for having been away so long.) In any case, Maynard had been under police surveillance for months, during which time the police were presumably investigating the murder, presumably picking up blacks and whites by the scores, and placing them in line-ups, and it seems never to have occurred to them to connect Maynard with the murder. Incidentally, the white assailant disappears completely and forever from this investigation, as though he had never existed.

That, roughly, was the case until that moment, as it could be reconstructed from Germany. Time was to reveal several unnerving details, but this outline never changed. It was to prove important, later, that during this time Tony had been involved with two white women, one of whom, Giselle Nicole, claiming extreme police harassment, disappeared. The other, Mary Quinn, he married. They did not live happily ever after, and Mary Quinn's subsequent conduct was scarcely that of a loving wife.

According to the treaty between Germany and America, two classes of prisoners are not subject to extradition: political prisoners, and those facing the death penalty. Tony wanted to fight the extradition proceedings, for he was certain that he would be murdered on the way back home. This fear may strike the ordinary American as preposterous, in spite of what they themselves know concerning the violence which is the heritage and the scourge of their country. I could not, of course, agree with Tony, but I didn't find his terror, which was exceedingly controlled and therefore very moving, in the least preposterous. But I had no remote motion how to go about fighting his extradition. Ironically, the very greatest obstacle lay in the fact that New York had abolished the death penalty. The plea could be made, then, only on political grounds. I agree with the Black Panther position concerning black prisoners: not one of them has ever had a fair trial, for not one of them has ever been tried by a jury of his peers. White middle-class America is always the jury, and they know absolutely nothing about the lives of the people on whom they sit in judgment: and this fact is not altered, on the contrary it is rendered more implacable by the presence of one or two black faces in the jury box.

But it would be difficult indeed to convey to a German court the political implications of a black man's arrest: difficult if not impossible to convey, especially to a nation "friendly" to the United States, to what extent black Americans are political prisoners. Muhammad Ali, formerly Cassius Clay, is a vivid example of what can happen to a black man who obeys the American injunction, *be true to your faith,* but his press has been so misleading that he is also an unwieldy and intimidating example. Muhammad Ali is one of the best of the "bad niggers" and has been publicly hanged like one, but since I had to avoid the religious issue, which had nothing to do with Tony's case, I could not cite him an example. Neither was the Maynard case likely to interest civil rights organizations, or the NAACP; it was, in fact, simply another example of a black hustler being thrown into jail. The complex of reasons dictating such a fate could scarcely be articulated in a letter to the German court. There was also the enormous and delicate problem of publicity. Though I had no choice in the matter, for I certainly couldn't abandon him, I was terrified that my presence in the case would work strongly to Tony's disadvantage. I intended to fight the extradition proceedings as hard as I knew how, but I knew how unlikely it was that we would win. In the event that we lost, Tony would be brought to trial and any publicity prior to that trial could certainly be considered prejudicial. On the other hand, both Tony and my German editor felt that an appeal to the press would work strongly in Tony's favor. It is really rather awful to find oneself in a position in which any move one makes may result in irreparable harm to another, and I was torn in two by this question for some time. But the question was brutally taken out of my hands.

One dark, Gothic evening, much delayed by the fact that we had spent hours trying to arrive at a strategy —no easy matter if one's strategy must be dictated by the laws of two different countries, and the psychology of two not so very different peoples—the German lawyer, my German editor, and myself, arrived at the door of the Holstenglacis prison. *We* were rattled because, though we were not exactly late, we knew that we were arriving at just about the time that prisoners were due to be taken upstairs for meals; and, furthermore, again a trick accomplished by my German publishers, by this time Tony and I no longer met in the public waiting room, but in another, smaller and private, where we could smoke, where we could talk. This was an enormous concession, and being late could possibly mean losing it.

Only the lawyer and I had passes to enter. My German editor—Fritz Raddadtz, an anti-Nazi German, who has the scars to prove it—had no right to enter at all. But the guard who opened the door also seemed rattled and, without examining anybody's pass, led us all into the room in which he knew I always awaited Tony.

And there we waited, for quite some time. Another rattled functionary appeared, explaining that Tony was not in his cell and could not be seen that night. My German editor, smelling a rat—I didn't, yet, and the lawyer seemed bewildered—pointed out that Tony, in his cell or not, was, nevertheless, somewhere in the prison, and that we were perfectly prepared to wait in this room until morning, or for weeks, if it came to that: that we would not, in short, leave until we saw Tony. The rattled functionary disappeared again. Then, after quite a long while, they brought in the birthday boy.

Someone had goofed in that prison, very badly; after this visit, heads surely rolled. Tony had been beaten, and beaten very hard; his cheekbones had disappeared and one of his eyes was crooked; he looked swollen above the neck, and he took down his shirt collar, presently, to show us the swelling on his shoulders. And he was weeping, trying not to—I had seen him with tears in his eyes, but I had never seen him weeping.

But when I say that heads surely rolled and that someone had goofed, I do not mean that they goofed because they beat him. They goofed because they let us see him. No one would have taken my word for this beating, or our lawyer's word. But Fritz knows what it means to be beaten in prison. And he, therefore, not only alerted the German press, but armed with the weight of one of the most powerful of German publishing houses, sued the German state. So, there it was, after all, anyway, in the newspapers, and I, too, had to meet the press.

———————

"I've got a religious medallion," Tony said—he has become a kind of Muslim, or, at least, an anti-Christian —"and the guard told me the other day that they were going to let me have it back again. Because they took it, you know. And I wanted it back. It means a lot to me—I'm not about to kill myself with it, I'm not about to kill myself. So, when the guard walked in, I asked him for it because he said he would bring it to me Friday night." (And this was Friday.) "Well, I don't know, he jumped salty and he walked out. And I started beating on the door of my cell, trying to make him come back, to listen to me, at least to explain to me *why* I couldn't have it, after he'd promised. And then the door opened and fifteen men walked in and they beat me up—fifteen men!"

The headline on one of the German newspapers, which, incongruously or cunningly enough also has beneath the headline an old photograph of myself, laughing, is: "Tony Never Lies"! This means at least two things, for it is not humanly possible for it to mean what it says. It means that Tony has never lied to me, though I have frequently watched him attempt to delude me into his delusions: but we human beings do this with each other all the time. Friends and lovers are able, sometimes, not always, to resist and correct the delusions. But it also means something exceedingly difficult to capture, which is that some people are liars, and some people are not. We will return to this speculation later. Somewhere in the Bible there is the chilling observation: *Ye are liars, and the truth's not in you.*

———————

I had been in London when Malcolm was murdered. The sister who worked for me then, Gloria, had the habit, whenever she decided that it was time to get me out of town, of simply arbitrarily picking up an invitation, it scarcely mattered to where, and putting me on a plane; so, for example, we once found ourselves in the midnight sun of Helsinki. This time, we were the guests of my British publishers, in London, and we were staying at the Hilton. On this particular night, we were free and we had decided to treat ourselves to a really fancy, friendly dinner. There we were, at the table, all dressed up, and we'd ordered everything, and we were having a very nice time with each other. The headwaiter came, and said there was a phone call for me, and Gloria rose to take it. She was very strange when she came back—she didn't say anything, and I began to be afraid to ask her anything. Then, nibbling at something she obviously wasn't tasting, she said,

"Well, I've got to tell you because the press is on its way over here. They've just killed Malcolm X."

The British press said that I accused innocent people of this murder. What I tried to say then, and will try to repeat now, is that whatever hand pulled the trigger did not buy the bullet. That bullet was forged in the crucible of the West, that death was dictated by the most successful conspiracy in the history of the world, and its name is white supremacy.

Years and years and years ago, a black friend of mine killed himself partly because of what he had been forced to endure at the hands of his countrymen because he was in love with a white girl. I had been away and didn't know that he was dead. I came out of the subway one evening, at West 4th Street, just as the train came in on the other side of the platform. A man I knew came running down the steps to catch this train. He saw me, and he yelled, "Did you hear what happened to Gene?" "No," I cried, "what happened?" "He's dead," shouted the hurrying man, and the subway doors closed and the train pulled out of the station.

When George Bernard Shaw wrote *Saint Joan*, he had the immense advantage of having never known her. He had never seen her walk, never heard her talk, could never have been haunted by any of those infinitesimal, inimitable tones, turns, tics, quirks, which are different in every human being, and which make love and death such inexorably private affairs. He had the advantage of the historical panorama: the forces responsible for Joan's death, as well as the ways in which she herself was responsible, were ranged as clearly as chessmen on a chessboard. The forces responsible for that death, and the forces released by it, had had a long time to make themselves felt, and, while Joan was a riddle for her time, she was not a riddle by the time Shaw got around to her: the riddle could be read in her effect in time. She had been safely burned, and somewhat more thoughtfully canonized and no longer posed any conceivable threat to anyone alive. She was, as Shaw points out, one of the world's first nationalists and terrified, equally, the feudal landlords and the princes of the church by refusing to concede their validity. They had no choice but to burn her, which did not, of course, by the merest iota, alter the exactness of her prophecy or the inevitability of their fate.

But it is a very different matter to attempt to deal with the present, in the present, and with a contemporary, younger than oneself, hideously dead too soon, and one who became, furthermore, long before he died, a much disputed legend. And there is, since his death, a Malcolm, virtually, for every persuasion. People who hated him, people who despised him, people who feared him, and people who, in their various ways and degrees, according to their various lights and darknesses, loved him, all claim him now. It is easy to claim him now, just as it was easy for the church to claim Saint Joan.

But, though this storm of human voices creates a great difficulty, it does not create the greatest one.

The greatest difficulty is to accept the fact that the man is dead. It is one thing to *know* that a friend is dead and another thing to accept, within oneself, that unanswering silence: that not many of us are able to accept the reality of death is both an obvious and a labyrynthine statement. The imagination, then, which has been assigned the job of recreating and interpreting a life one witnessed and loved simply kicks like a stalled motor, refuses to make contact, and will not get the vehicle to move. One no longer knows if one ever really knew the person, but, what's worse, that no longer makes any difference: one's stuck with whatever it is one thought one knew, with whatever filtered through the complex screen of one's limitations. That's one's legacy, that's all there is: and now only that work which is love and that love which is work will allow one to come anywhere near obeying the dictum laid down by the great Ray Charles, and—tell the truth.

_____

Every new environment, particularly if one knows that one must make the effort to accustom oneself to working in it, risks being more than a little traumatic. One finds oneself nervously examining one's new surroundings, searching for the terms of the adjustment;

therefore, in the beginning, I made a somewhat too conscious effort to be pleased by Hollywood. There was the sky, after all, which New Yorkers seldom see, and there was space, which New Yorkers have forgotten, there was the mighty and dramatic Pacific, there were the hills. Some very valuable and attractive people had lived and functioned here for years, I reminded myself, and there was really no reason why I could not—so I insisted to myself. I had a few friends and acquaintances here already, scattered from Watts to Baldwin Hills to Mulholland Drive, and I was sure they'd be happy if I decided to stay. If I were going to be in Hollywood for months, there was no point in raising the odds against me by hating it, or despising it; besides, such an attitude seemed too obvious a defense against my fear of it. As hotels go, the Beverly Hills is more congenial than most, and certainly everyone there was very nice to me. And so I tried—too hard—to look about me with wonder, and be pleased. But I was already in trouble, and the odds against the venture were very long odds indeed.

I was actually in the Beverly Hills until more permanent lodging could be found. This was not easy, since it involved finding someone to take care of me—to keep house, cook, and drive. *I* was no help, since I was still, at the beginning of 1968, committed to various fund-raising functions in the East, and, more particularly, to the question of a lawyer for Tony Maynard, who had been extradited from Germany and placed in

the Tombs, in New York. He had been extradited very
shortly after I left Hamburg, so speedily indeed that
I was unable to fly from the Coast to meet him in New
York, as I had promised. I had engaged, at his sugges-
tion, a lawyer named S. J. Siegel, a very sharp, spry old
man, who must have been close to eighty, and who was
to teach me a great deal about criminal lawyers. Part
of the irreducible conflict which was to drive both
Columbia and myself up the wall was already implicit
during those early days at the Beverly Hills hotel. The
conflict was simply between my life as a writer and my
life as—not spokesman exactly, but as public witness
to the situation of black people. I had to play both
roles: there was nothing anyone, including myself,
could do about it. This was an unprecedented situation for Columbia, which, after all, had me under exclusive contract and didn't really like my dashing off,
making public appearances. It was an unprecedented
situation for me, too, since I had never before been
under exclusive contract, and had always juggled my
conflicting schedules as best I could. I had lived with
my two roles for a long time, and had even, insofar as
this is ever true, begun to get used to them—I accepted, anyway, that the dichotomy wasn't likely to
end soon. But it didn't make the Hollywood scene any
easier. It wasn't a matter of wiping the slate clean of
existing commitments and then vanishing behind the
typewriter, nor was it even a matter of keeping outside
commitments to a minimum, though I tried: events

tioned, even by people who did not know who I was, or who thought I was Sammy Davis. It was simply taken for granted that I would not have been in the hotel if I had not belonged there. This, irrationally enough, got to me—*did* I belong there? In any case, thousands of black people, miles away, did *not* belong there, though some of them sometimes came to visit me there. (People had to come and get me, or come to visit me, because I do not drive.) The drive from Beverly Hills to Watts and back again is a long and loaded drive—I sometimes felt as though my body were being stretched across those miles. I don't think I felt anything so trivial as guilt, guilt at what appeared to be my comparative good fortune, I knew more about comparative fortunes than that, but I felt a stunning helplessness. These two worlds would never meet, and that fact prefigured disaster for my countrymen, and me. It caused me to look about me with an intensity of wonder which had no pleasure in it. Perhaps even more than the drive from Beverly Hills to Watts, the effect of this ruthless division was summed up for me by a visit I received from a young, very bright black man whom I had met years before, in Boston, after a lecture. Then, he had been very bright indeed, eager, full of ideas for his future, and the future of black people. A few years later, I had run across him, briefly, in Helsinki—he was studying, and seeing the world. Beautiful, I had thought then, make it, baby—it's wonderful to see a black cat at large in the world. Alas, to be at large in the world is also distinctly to risk being lost in it, and now, one afternoon, I received a message from a Prince of Abyssinia and I forget how many other territories, he was downstairs. In spite of the exotic titles, I recognized the domestic name, and I had him sent up. Here he came, then, a piteous, mad, unutterably moving wreck; he could scarcely have passed his thirtieth birthday. He wanted me to deposit ten thousand dollars in one of the many bank accounts he had around the world. He had a map, and a list of the banks, his patrons, and his titles, all impeccably handwritten. When confronting madness, it is usually best to hold one's peace, and so I do not know what I could have said. I did not question his titles, or his fortune, but indicated that I did not have ten thousand dollars. He took this with very good grace, had another drink, and bade me farewell—he had a pressing appointment with a fellow potentate. It was dark when he left, and black people—or white people, for that matter—walking in Beverly Hills do not walk far unnoticed. I almost started to call him a cab, but his regal bearing forbade it, and I then realized that there was nothing I could do.

I, of course, will always believe that this boy would not have been so quickly broken on the wheel of life if he had not been born black, in America. Many of my countrymen will not agree with me and will accuse me of special pleading. Neither they, nor I, can hope to come anywhere near the truth of the matter, so long as a man's color exerts so powerful a force on his fate. In the long meantime, I can only say that the authority of my countrymen in these matters is not equal to my own, since I know what black Americans endure—know it in my own flesh and spirit, know it by the human wreckage through which I have passed.

Therefore, my desire to be seduced, charmed, was a hope poisoned by despair: for better or for worse, it simply was not in me to make a separate peace. It was a symptom of how bitterly weary I was of wandering, how I hoped to find a resting place, reconciliation, in the land where I was born. But everything that might have charmed me merely reminded me of how many were excluded, how many were suffering and groaning and dying, not far from a paradise which was itself but another circle of hell. Everything that charmed me reminded me of someplace else, someplace where I could walk and talk, someplace where I was freer than I was at home, someplace where I could live without the stifling mask—made me homesick for a liberty I had never tasted here, and without which I could never live or work. In America, I was free only in battle, never free to rest—and he who finds no way to rest cannot long survive the battle.

Watts doesn't immediately look like a slum, if you come from New York; but it does if you drive from Beverly Hills. I have said that it is a very long drive, to elicit from—students at many splendid universities. The future leaders of this country (in principle, anyway) do not impress me as being the intellectual equals of the most despised among us. I am not being vindictive when I say that, nor am I being sentimental or chauvinistic; and indeed the reason that this would be so is a very simple one. It is only very lately that white students, in the main, have had any reason to question the structure into which they were born; it is the very lateness of the hour, and their bewildered resentment—their sense of having been betrayed— which is responsible for their romantic excesses; and a young, white revolutionary remains, in general, far more romantic than a black one. For it is a very different matter, and results in a very different intelligence, to grow up under the necessity of questioning everything—everything, from the question of one's identity to the literal, brutal question of how to save one's life in order to begin to live it. White children, in the main, and whether they are rich or poor, grow up with a grasp of reality so feeble that they can very accurately be described as deluded—about themselves and the world they live in. White people have managed to get through entire lifetimes in this euphoric state, but black people have not been so lucky: a black man who sees the world the way John Wayne, for example, sees it would not be an eccentric patriot, but a raving maniac. The reason for this, at bottom, is that the doctrine of white supremacy, which still controls most white people, is itself a stupendous delusion: but to be born black in America is an immediate, a mortal challenge. People who cling to their delusions find it difficult, if not impossible, to learn anything worth learning: a people under the necessity of creating themselves must examine everything, and soak up learning the way the roots of a tree soak up water. A people still held in bondage must believe that *Ye shall know the truth, and the truth shall make ye free.*

But, of course, what black people are also learning as they learn is the truth about white people: and that's the rub. Actually, black people have known the truth about white people for a long time, but now there is no longer any way for the truth to be hidden. The whole world knows it. The truth which frees black people will also free white people, but this is a truth which white people find very difficult to swallow.

They need desperately to be released, for one thing, from the necessity of lying all the time. I remember visiting a correctional school in Watts where the boys were being taught a "useful" trade. I visited some of the shops—they were being taught to make wooden frames for hassocks—nonsense like that. The boys knew it was a bullshit trip, the teachers knew it, the principal, escorting me through the school, knew it. He looked ashamed of himself, and he should have been ashamed. The truth is that this country does not know what to do with its black population now that the blacks are no longer a source of wealth, are no longer to be bought and sold and bred, like cattle; and they especially do not know what to do with young black men, who pose as devastating a threat to the economy as they do to the morals of young white cheerleaders. It is not at all accidental that the jails and the army and the needle claim so many, but there are still too many prancing about for the public comfort. Americans will, of course, deny, with horror, that they are dreaming of anything like "the final solution"—those Americans, that is, who are likely to be asked: what goes on in the great, vast, private hinterland of the American heart can only be guessed at by observing the way the country goes these days. Some pale, compelling nightmare —an overwhelming collection of private nightmares— is responsible for the irresponsible ferocity of the Omnibus Crime Control and Safe Streets Act. Some vindictive terror on the part of the people made possible the Government's indefensible and obscene performance in Chicago. Something has gone violently wrong in a nation when the government dares attempt to muzzle the press—a press already quite supine enough—and to intimidate reporters by the use of the subpoena. Black men have been burned alive in this country more than once—many men now living have seen it with their own eyes; black men and boys are being murdered here today, in cold blood, and with impunity; and it is a very serious matter when the government which is sworn to protect the interests of all American citizens publicly and unabashedly allies itself with the enemies of black men. Let us tell it like it is: the rhetoric of a Stennis, a Maddox, a Wallace, historically and actually, has brought death to untold numbers of black people and it was meant to bring death to them. This is absolutely true, no matter who denies it—no black man can possibly deny it. Now, in the interest of the public peace, it is the Black Panthers who are being murdered in their beds, by the dutiful and zealous police. But, for a policeman, all black men, especially young black men, are probably Black Panthers and all black women and children are probably allied with them: just as, in a Vietnamese village, the entire population, men, women, children, are considered as probable Vietcong. In the village, as in the ghetto, those who were not dangerous before the search-and-destroy operation assuredly become so afterward, for the inhabitants of the village, like the inhabitants of the ghetto, realize that they are identified, judged, menaced, murdered, solely because of the color of their skin. This is as curious a way of waging a war for a people's freedom as it is of maintaining the domestic public peace.

The ghetto, beleaguered, betrayed by Washington, by the total lack of vision of the men in Washington, determined to outwit, withstand, survive, this present, overwhelming danger, yet lacks a focus, a rallying point, a spokesman. And many of us looked at each other and sighed, saying, *Lord, we really need Malcolm now.*

Hollywood, or a segment of it, at least, was becoming increasingly active on the question of civil rights —now, I thought, sourly, and somewhat unjustly, that the question had been rendered moribund. Just the same, there was a groundswell to replace the toothsome, grimly folksy mayor, Sam Yorty, who had been in office since 1911, with someone who had heard of the twentieth century, in this case, Tom Bradley, a Negro. People like Jack Lemmon, Jean Seberg, Robert Culp, and France Nuyen were actively supporting Martin Luther King, pledging money and getting others to pledge, and some were helping to raise money for a projected Malcolm X Foundation.

Marlon Brando was very much in the forefront of all this. He had a strong interest in the Black Panthers and was acquainted with many of them. On April 6, Eldridge Cleaver was wounded, and Bobby Hutton was killed, in Oakland, in what the police describe as a "shoot-out." Marlon called me to say that he was going up to Oakland. I wanted to go with him, but Martin Luther King had been murdered two days before, and, to tell the truth, I was in a state resembling shock. I can't describe this, or defend it, and I won't dwell on it. Marlon flew up to Oakland to deliver the eulogy for seventeen-year-old Bobby Hutton, shot down, exactly, by the dutiful police, like a mad dog in the streets. The Oakland Police Force was outraged, naturally, and I think they threatened to sue him, probably for defamation of character. The Grand Jury had judged their shooting of an unarmed, black adolescent as "justifiable homicide": the names of these jurors, many of whom can claim as their intimates eminent judges and lawyers, could scarcely have been found on the Master Panel if it were supposed that they were capable of bringing in any other verdict.

(I went to Oakland to visit the house where Hutton was killed, and Cleaver wounded. The house where the Panthers were is wedged between two houses just like it. There are windows on either side of the house, facing the alley; facing the street, there is only an enormous garage door, from which, needless to say, no one could hope to shoot, and live. The house, particularly the basement, where the people were, looks like something from a search-and-destroy operation. The warehouse across the street, where the cops were, doesn't have a scratch on it: so much for the official concept of a shoot-out. When I was there, there were flowers on a rock, marking the spot where Bobby fell: the people of the neighborhood had made of the place a shrine.)

I think it was in March, but it may have been somewhat earlier, that Martin Luther King came to town, to speak in a private dwelling in the Hollywood hills to raise money for the Southern Christian Leadership Conference. I had not seen Martin in quite some time, and I looked forward to seeing him in a setting where we might be able to talk a little bit before he had to dash off and grab some sleep before catching the next plane. For years, most of us had seen each other only at airports, or, wearily, marching, marching.

It always seems—unfairly enough, perhaps, in many cases—incongruous and suspect when relatively wealthy and certainly very wordly people come together for the express purpose of declaring their allegiance to a worthy cause and with the intention of parting with some of their money. I think that someone like myself can scarcely avoid a certain ambivalence before such a spectacle—someone like myself being someone significantly and crucially removed from the world which produced these people. In my own experience, genuine, disinterested compassion or conviction are very rare; yet, it is as well to remember that, rare as these are, they are real, they exist. Giving these people the benefit of the necessary doubt —assuming, that is, for example, that if they were called to serve on a Grand Jury investigating the legal murder of a black, they would have the courage to vote their conscience instead of their class—I would hazard that, in the case of most people in gatherings such as these, their presence is due to a vivid, largely incoherent uneasiness. They are nagged by a sense that something is terribly wrong, and that they must do what they can to put it right: but much of their quality, or lack of it, depends on what they perceive to be wrong.

134

They do not, in any case, know what to do—who does? it may be asked—and so they give their money and their allegiance to whoever appears to be doing what they feel should be done. Their fatal temptation, to which, mostly, they appear to succumb, is to assume that they are, then, off the hook. But, on the other hand, always assuming that they are serious, the crucial lack in their perception is that they do not quite see where, when the chips are down, their allegiance is likely to land them—*à la lanterne!* or to recantation: they do not know how ruthless and powerful is the evil that lives in the world. Years before, for example, I remember having an argument—a most melancholy argument—with a friend of mine concerning our relation to Martin. It was shortly after our celebrated and stormy meeting with Bobby Kennedy, and I was very low. I said that we could petition and petition and march and march and raise money and give money until we wore ourselves out and the stars began to moan: none of this endeavor would or could reach the core of the matter, it would change nobody's fate. The thirty thousand dollars raised tonight would be gone in bail bonds in the morning, and so it would continue until we dropped. Nothing would ever reach the conscience of the people of this nation—it was a dream to suppose that the people of any nation had a conscience. Some individuals within the nation might, and the nation always saw to it that these people came to a bad, if not a bloody end. Nothing we could do would prevent, at last, an open confrontation. And where, then, when the chips were down, would we stand?

We were seated near a fireplace, and my friend's face was very thoughtful. He looked over at me, almost as though he were seeing me for the first time.

"You really believe that, don't you?"

I said, "I wish I didn't. But I'm afraid I do."

"Well," he said, at last, "if you're black, you don't have to worry too much about where you stand. They've got *that* covered, I believe."

Indeed, they do. And, therefore, people like the people in the Hollywood hills can be looked on as the highly problematical leaven in the loaf. Instinctively, when speaking before them, one attempts to fan into a blaze, or at least into positive heat, their somewhat chilled apprehension of life. In attempting to lessen the distance between them and oneself, one is also, unconsciously and inevitably, suggesting that they lessen the distance between themselves and their deepest hopes and fears and desires; even that they dispense with that middleman they call doctor, who is one of their greatest, most infantile self-indulgences. One senses sometimes in their still faces an intense, speculative hesitation. Bobby Seale insists that one of the things that most afflict white people is their disastrous concept of God; they have never accepted the dark gods, and their fear of the dark gods, who live in them at least as surely as the white God does, causes them to distrust life. It causes them, profoundly, to be fascinated by, and more than a little frightened of the lives led by black people: it is this tension which makes them problematical. But, on the other hand, it must be becoming increasingly clear to some, at least, that all of us are standing in the same deep shadow, a shadow which can only be lifted by human courage and honor. Many still hope to keep their honor and their safety, too. No one can blame them for this hope, it is impossible indeed not to share it: but when queried as to the soundness of such a hope, for a people caught in a civilization in crisis, history fails to give any very sanguine answers.

Eventually, Martin arrived, in a light blue suit, accompanied by Andrew Young, and they both looked very tired. We were very glad to see each other. We sat down in a relatively secluded corner and tried to bring each other up to date.

Alas, it would never be possible for us to bring each other up to date. We had first met during the last days of the Montgomery bus boycott—and how long ago was that? It was senseless to say, eight years, ten years ago—it was longer ago than time can reckon. Martin and I had never got to know each other well, circumstances, if not temperament, made that impossible, but I had much respect and affection for him, and I think Martin liked me, too. I told him what I was doing in Hollywood, and both he and Andrew, looking perhaps a trifle dubious, wished me well. I don't remember whether it was on this evening that we arranged to appear together a few weeks later at Carnegie Hall, or if this had already been arranged. Presently, Marlon, very serious, and even being, as I remember, a little harsh with the assembled company—wanting to make certain that they understood the utter gravity of our situation, and the speed with which the time for peaceful change was running out—took the floor, and introduced Dr. Martin Luther King, Jr.

As our situation had become more complex, Martin's speeches had become simpler and more concrete. As I remember, he spoke very simply that evening on the work of the Southern Christian Leadership Conference, what had been done, what was being done, and the enormity of the tasks that lay ahead. But I remember his tone more than his words. He spoke very humbly, as one of many workers, speaking to his co-workers. I think he made everyone in that room feel that whatever they were doing, whatever they could do, was important, was of the utmost importance. He did not flatter them—very subtly, he challenged them, challenged them to live up to their moral obligations. The room was quite remarkable when he finished—still, thoughtful, grateful: perhaps, in the most serious sense of that weary phrase, profoundly honored.

And yet—how striking to compare his tone that night with what it had been not many years before! Not many years before, we had all marched on Washington. Something like two hundred and fifty thousand people had come to the nation's capital to petition their government for a redress of grievances. They had come from all over the nation, in every condition, in every conceivable attire, and in all kinds of vehicles. Even a skeptic like myself, with every reason to doubt that the petition would, or could, be heard, or acted on, could not fail to respond to the passion of so many people, gathered together, for that purpose, in that place. Their passion made one forget that a terrified Washington had bolted its doors and fled, that many politicians had been present only because they had been afraid not to be, that John Lewis, then of SNCC, had been forced to tone down his speech because of the insuperable arrogance of a Boston archbishop, that the administration had done everything in its power to prevent the March, even to finding out if I, who had nothing whatever to do with the March as organized, would use my influence to try to prevent it. (I said that such influence as I had, which wasn't much, would certainly not be used against the March, and, perhaps to prove this, I led the March on Washington from the American Church, in Paris, to the American Embassy, and brought back from Paris a scroll bearing about a thousand names. I wonder where it is now.)

In spite of all that one knew, and feared, it was a very stirring day, and one very nearly dared, in spite of all that one knew, to hope—to hope that the need and the passion of the people, so nakedly and vividly, and with such dignity revealed, would not be, once again, betrayed. (The People's Republic of China had sent a telegram in our support, which was repudiated by Roy Wilkins, who said, in effect, that we would be glad to accept such a telegram on the day that the Chinese were allowed to petition *their* government for redress of grievances, as we were petitioning ours. I had an uneasy feeling that we might live to hear this boast ring somewhat mockingly in our ears.)

But Martin had been quite moving that day. Marlon (carrying a cattle prod, for the purpose of revealing the depravity of the South) and Sidney Poitier and Harry Belafonte, Charlton Heston, and some others of us had been called away to do a Voice of America show for Ed Murrow, and so we watched and listened to Martin on television. All of us were very silent in that room, listening to Martin, feeling the passion of the people flowing up to him and transforming him, transforming us. Martin finished with one hand raised: "Free at last, free at last, praise God Almighty, I'm free at last!" That day, for a moment, it almost seemed that we stood on a height, and could see our inheritance; perhaps we could make the kingdom real, perhaps the beloved community would not forever remain that dream one dreamed in agony. The people quietly dispersed at nightfall, as had been agreed. Sidney Poitier took us out to dinner that night, in a very, very quiet Washington. The people had come to their capitol, had made themselves known, and were gone: no one could any longer doubt that their suffering was real.

Ironically enough, after Washington, I eventually went on the road, on a lecture tour which carried me to Hollywood. So I was in Hollywood when, something like two weeks later, my phone rang, and a nearly hysterical, white, female CORE worker told me that a Sunday school in Birmingham had been bombed, and that four young black girls had been blown into eternity. That was the first answer we received to our petition.

The original plans for the March on Washington had been far from polite: the original plan had been to lie down on airport runways, to block the streets and offices, to immobilize the city completely, and to remain as long as we had to, to force the government to recognize the urgency and the justice of our demands. Malcolm was very caustic about the March on Washington, which he described as a sell-out. I think he was right. Martin, five years later, was five years wearier and five years sadder, and still petitioning. But the impetus was gone, because the people no longer believed in their petitions, no longer believed in their government. The reasoning behind the March on Washington, as it eventually evolved—or as it was, in Malcolm's words, "diluted"—was that peaceful assembly would produce the best results. But, five years later, it was very hard to believe that the frontal assault, as planned, on the capitol, could possibly have produced more bloodshed, or more despair. Five years later, it seemed clear that we had merely postponed, and not at all to our advantage, the hour of dreadful reckoning.

Martin and Andrew and I said good night to each other, and promised to meet in New York.

———————

Siegel, the first lawyer I engaged for Tony, was a refugee from *Bleak House,* and I wish I'd met him in those pages and not in life. Spry, as I have said, white-haired, cunning, with a kind of old-fashioned, phony courtliness, he was eventually to make me think of vultures. He had been a criminal lawyer for a long time, practically since birth, and he had, I was told, a "good" reputation. But I was to discover that to have a "good" reputation as a criminal lawyer does not necessarily reflect any credit on said lawyer's competence or dedication; still less does it indicate that he has any interest in his clients: the term seems to refer almost exclusively to the lawyer's ability to wheel and deal and to his influence with other lawyers and judges, and district attorneys. A criminal lawyer's reputation—except, of course, for the one or two titans in the field—would appear to depend on his standing in this club. The fate of his client depends, to put it brutally, on the client's money: one may say, generally, that, if a poor man in trouble with the law receives justice, one can suppose heavenly intervention.

A poor man is always an isolated man, in the sense that his intimates are as ignorant and as helpless as he.

Tony has been in prison since October 27, 1967, and remains in prison still. He had been brought to trial once in all that time; the trial resulted in a hung jury. A citizen more favorably placed than Tony would never have been treated in this way. It would appear, for example, that Tony's constitutional rights were violated at the very moment he was arrested because of the means used to identify him. This question has never been brought up, though Tony has insisted on it time and again. The police are very sensitive about being accused of violating a suspect's constitutional rights—they are, indeed, as sensitive to any and all criticism as aging beauty queens—and would never have arrested Tony in the way that they did if they had not been certain that his accusation could never be heard. Tony had almost nothing going for him, except his devoted sister, Valerie, and me. But neither Valerie nor I are equipped to deal with the world into which we found ourselves so suddenly plunged, and I found myself severely handicapped in this battle by being forced to fight it from three thousand miles away.

This meant that there was a vacuum where Tony's witness should have been. This would not have been so if the system worked differently, or if it were served by different people. But the system works as it works, and it attracts the people it attracts. The poor, the black, and the ignorant become the stepping stones of careers; for the people who make up this remarkable club are judged by their number of arrests and convictions. These matter far more than justice, if justice can be said to matter at all. It is clearly much easier to drag some ignorant wretch to court and burden him with whatever crimes one likes than it is to undergo the inconvenience and possible danger of finding out what actually happened, and who is actually guilty. In my experience, the defenders of the public peace do not care who is guilty. I have been arrested by the New York police, for example, and charged guilty before the judge, and had the charge entered in the record, without anyone asking me how I chose to plead, and without being allowed to speak. (I had the case thrown out of court, and if I'd had any means, I would have sued the city. The judge, when asked to explain his oversight, said that the court was crowded that day, and that the traffic noises, coming in from the streets, distracted him.)

In Tony Maynard's case, the question of justice is simply mocked when one considers that no attempt appears to have been made to discover the white assailant, and also by the fact that Tony has been asked to plead guilty and promised a light sentence if he would so plead. I know this to be a fact because, during Tony's trial, while the jury was out—and the jury was out much longer than anyone expected it to be— Galena, the D.A. who was prosecuting Tony, took me aside, in the presence of Tony's sister, Valerie, and the second lawyer I engaged for Tony, Selig Lenefsky, to ask me to use my influence to persuade Tony to accept the deal. He also told me that they would "get" him, anyway. Lenefsky and Galena are partners now, a perfectly normal development, which enhances the respectful trust and affection with which the poor regard their protectors.

But I anticipate. My absence from New York meant that there was virtually no pressure on Siegel, and Siegel, as far as I could discover, did nothing whatever. Most of his correspondence with me mentions money. I had paid him a retainer, and I wasn't trying to beat him out of his fee; but I was naturally reluctant, especially as time wore on, with no progress being made, to continue throwing good money after bad. This led, really, to a stalemate, and Valerie and I found ourselves thoroughly at a loss. I wanted to fire Siegel, but on what basis would I hire the next lawyer? No one I knew knew anything about criminal lawyers; the lawyers I knew dismissed them as a "scurvy breed." I thought of Melvin Belli, but he operates in California; I thought of Louis Nizer, and, in fact, tried to see him: but I knew I couldn't pay the fee for either of these lawyers. I thought of publicity, but it is not so easy to get publicity for a case which is, alas, so unremarkable. I didn't feel that my unsupported testimony would mean very much, and I couldn't get the groundswell going which might lead to a public hue and cry. I couldn't work at it full time because I was under contract in California and had to get back there. And, furthermore, I now had to finish that screenplay, if only to collect my fee: what price justice indeed!

Val and I would meet in Siegel's office, to learn that the trial had been postponed again, but that this might be all to the good because it meant that Judge So-and-So instead of Judge What-not would be sitting—at least, he would try to make certain that it was Judge What-not instead of Judge So-and-So. He, Siegel, was on friendly terms with Judge What-not, he'd call him later in the evening. And he would smile in a very satisfied way, as though to say, You see how I'm putting myself out for you, how much I take your interests to heart. No, his private investigators had failed to locate Dennis Morris. (Morris is the unknown who identified Tony by means of a photograph.) Morris had disappeared. No one seemed to know where he was. No, there was no word about the whereabouts of Michael Crist, either. All of this took time and money —and he would light a cigar, his bright blue eyes watching me expectantly.

Well, what in the world could we say to this terrifying old man? How could we know whether he had spoken to a single person, or made the remotest phone call on Tony's behalf? We could spend the rest of our lives in this office, while Tony was perishing in jail, and never know. He didn't care about Tony, but we hadn't expected him to—we had supposed that he cared about something else. What? his honor as a criminal lawyer? Probably—which proved what fools we were. His honor as a criminal lawyer was absolutely unassailable, he was a lifetime member of the club. We had no way whatever of lighting a fire under his ass and making him do what we were paying him to do. He didn't need us. There were thousands like us, yes, and black like us, who would keep him in cigars forever, turning over their nickels and dimes to get their loved ones out of trouble. And sometimes he would get them out—he had no objection to getting people out of trouble. But it was a lottery; it depended on whose number came up; and he certainly wasn't bucking the machine. Day after day after day, we would leave him and go to the Tombs, and I would see Tony: who was bearing up fantastically well; I'd not have believed he could be so tough. Seeing him, I felt guilty, frustrated, and helpless, felt time flowing through my hands like water. Val would be waiting for me when I came down, we might walk around a bit, and then I would leave her with the others, who were waiting for the six o'clock visit.

Whoever wishes to know who is in prison in this country has only to go to the prisons and watch who comes to visit. We spent hours and hours, days and days, eternities, down at the Tombs, Val and I, and, later, my brother, David. I suppose there must have been white visitors; it stands, so to speak, to reason, but they were certainly overwhelmed by the dark, dark mass. Black, and Puerto Rican matrons, black, and Puerto Rican girls, black, and Puerto Rican boys, black, and Puerto Rican men: such are the fish trapped

147

in the net called justice. Bewilderment, despair, and poverty roll through the halls like a smell: the visitors have come, looking for a miracle. The miracle will be to find someone who really cares about the people in prison. But no one can afford to care. The prison is overcrowded, the calendars full, the judges busy, the lawyers ambitious, and the cops zealous. What does it matter if someone gets trapped here for a year or two, gets ruined here, goes mad here, commits murder or suicide here? It's too bad, but that's the way the cookie crumbles sometimes.

I do not claim that everyone in prison here is innocent, but I do claim that the law, as it operates, is guilty, and that the prisoners, therefore, are all unjustly imprisoned. Is it conceivable, after all, that any middle-class white boy—or, indeed, almost any white boy—would have been arrested on so grave a charge as murder, with such flimsy substantiation, and forced to spend, as of this writing, three years in prison? What force, precisely, is operating when a prisoner is advised, requested, ordered, intimidated, or forced, to confess to a crime he has not committed, and promised a lighter sentence for so perjuring and debasing himself? Does the law exist for the purpose of furthering the ambitions of those who have sworn to uphold the law, or is it seriously to be considered as a moral, unifying force, the health and strength of a nation? The trouble with these questions, of course, is that they sound rhetorical, and have the effect of irritating

forever, a bright day. I had moved there from the Beverly Hills Hotel, into a house the producer had found for me. Billy Dee Williams had come to town, and he was staying at the house; and a lot of the day had been spent with a very bright, young, lady reporter, who was interviewing me about the film version of Malcolm. I felt very confident that day—I was never to feel so confident again—and I talked very freely to the reporter. (Too freely, Marvin Worth, the producer, was to tell me later.) I had decided to lay my cards on the table and to state, as clearly as I could, what I felt the movie was about and how I intended to handle it. I thought that this might make things simpler later on, but I was wrong about that. The studio and I were at loggerheads, really, from the moment I stepped off the plane. Anyway, I had opted for candor, or a reasonable facsimile of same, and sounded as though I were in charge of the film, as, indeed, by my lights, for that moment, certainly, I had to be. I was really in a difficult position because, by both temperament and experience, I tend to work alone, and I dread making announcements concerning my work. But I was in a very public position, and I thought that I had better make my own announcements rather than have them made for me. The studio, on the other hand, did not want me making announcements of any kind at all. So there we were, and this particular tension, since it got to the bloody heart of the matter— the question of by whose vision, precisely, this film was to be controlled—was not to be resolved until I finally threw up my hands and walked away.

I very much wanted Billy Dee for Malcolm, and since no one else had any other ideas, I didn't see why this couldn't work out. In brutal Hollywood terms, Poitier is the only really big, black box-office star, and this fact, especially since Marvin had asked me to "keep an eye out" for an actor, gave me, as I considered it, a free hand. To tell the bitter truth, from the very first days we discussed it, I had never had any intention of allowing the Columbia brass to cast this part: I was determined to take my name off the production if I were overruled. Call this bone-headed stupidity, or insufferable arrogance, or what you will—I had made my decision, and once I had made it, nothing could make me waver, and nothing could make me alter it. If there were errors in my concept of the film, and if I made errors in the execution, well, then, I would have to pay for my errors. But one can learn from one's errors. What one cannot survive is allowing other people to make your errors for you, discarding your own vision, in which, at least, you believe, for someone else's vision, in which you do *not* believe.

Anyway, all that shit had yet to hit the fan. This day, the girl, and Billy, and I had a few drinks by the swimming pool. Walter, my cook-chauffeur, was about to begin preparing supper. The girl got up to leave, and we walked her to her car, and came back to the swimming pool, jubilant.

The phone had been brought out to the pool, and now it rang. Billy was on the other side of the pool, doing what I took to be African improvisations to the sound of Aretha Franklin. And I picked up the phone.

It was David Moses. It took awhile before the sound of his voice—I don't mean the *sound* of his voice, something *in* his voice—got through to me.

He said, "Jimmy—? Martin's just been shot," and I don't think I said anything, or felt anything. I'm not sure I knew who *Martin* was. Yet, though I know—or I think—the record player was still playing, silence fell. David said, "He's not dead yet"—*then* I knew who Martin was—"but it's a head wound—so—"

I don't remember what I said; obviously, I must have said something. Billy and Walter were watching me. I told them what David had said.

I hardly remember the rest of that evening at all, it's retired into some deep cavern in my mind. We must have turned on the television set, if we had one, I don't remember. But we must have had one. I remember weeping, briefly, more in helpless rage than in sorrow, and Billy trying to comfort me. But I really don't remember that evening at all. Later, Walter told me that a car had prowled around the house all night.

The very last time I saw Medgar Evers, he stopped at his house on the way to the airport so I could autograph my books for him and his wife and children. I remember Myrilie Evers standing outside, smiling, and we waved, and Medgar drove to the airport and put me on the plane. He grinned that kind of country boy preacher's grin of his, and we said we'd see each other soon.

Months later, I was in Puerto Rico, working on the last act of my play. My host and hostess, and my friend, Lucien, and I, had spent a day or so wandering around the island, and now we were driving home. It was a wonderful, bright, sunny day, the top to the car was down, we were laughing and talking, and the radio was playing. Then the music stopped, and a voice announced that Medgar Evers had been shot to death in the carport of his home, and his wife and children had seen that big man fall.

No, I can't describe it. I've thought of it often, or been haunted by it often. I said something like, "That's a friend of mine—!" but no one in the car really knew who he was, or what he had meant to me, and to so many people. For some reason, I didn't see him: I saw Myrilie, and the children. They were quite small children. The blue sky seemed to descend like a blanket, and the speed of the car, the wind against my face, seemed stifling, as though the elements were determined to stuff something down my throat, to fill me with something I could never contain. And I couldn't say anything, I couldn't cry; I just remembered his face, a bright, blunt, handsome face, and his weariness, which he wore like his skin, and the way he said *ro-aad* for road, and his telling me how the tatters

153

of clothes from a lynched body hung, flapping, in the tree for days, and how he had to pass that tree every day. Medgar. Gone.

I went to Atlanta alone, I do not remember why. I wore the suit I had bought for my Carnegie Hall appearance with Martin. I seem to have had the foresight to have reserved a hotel room, for I vaguely remember stopping in the hotel and talking to two or three preacher type looking men, and we started off in the direction of the church. We had not got far before it became very clear that we would never get anywhere near it. We went in this direction and then in that direction, but the press of people choked us off. I began to wish that I had not come incognito, and alone, for now that I was in Atlanta, I wanted to get inside the church. I lost my companions and sort of squeezed my way, inch by inch, closer to the church. But, directly between me and the church, there was an impassable wall of people. Squeezing my way up to this point, I had considered myself lucky to be small; but now my size worked against me, for, though there were people on the church steps who knew me, whom I knew, they could not possibly see me, and I could not shout. I squeezed a few more inches and asked a very big man ahead of me please to let me through. He moved, and said, "Yeah, let me see you get through this big Cadillac." It was true—there it was, smack in front of me, big as a house. I saw Jim Brown at a distance, but he didn't see me. I leaned up on the car, making frantic signals, and, finally, someone on the church steps did see me and came to the car and sort of lifted me over. I talked to Jim Brown for a minute, and then somebody led me into the church and I sat down.

The church was packed, of course, incredibly so. Far in the front, I saw Harry Belafonte sitting next to Coretta King. I had interviewed Coretta years ago, when I was doing a profile on her husband. We had got on very well; she had a nice, free laugh. Ralph David Abernathy sat in the pulpit. I remembered him from years ago, sitting in his shirtsleeves in the house in Montgomery, big, black, and cheerful, pouring some cool soft drink, and, later, getting me settled in a nearby hotel. In the pew directly before me sat Marlon Brando, Sammy Davis, Eartha Kitt—covered in black, looking like a lost ten-year-old girl—and Sidney Poitier, in the same pew, or nearby. Marlon saw me and nodded. The atmosphere was black, with a tension indescribable—as though something, perhaps the heavens, perhaps the earth, might crack. Everyone sat very still.

The actual service sort of washed over me, in waves. It wasn't that it seemed unreal; it was the most real church service I've ever sat through in my life, or ever hope to sit through; but I have a childhood hangover thing about not weeping in public, and I was concentrating on holding myself together. I did not want to weep for Martin; tears seemed futile. But I may also have been afraid, and I could not have been the only one, that if I began to weep, I would not be able to stop. There was more than enough to weep for, if one was to weep—so many of us, cut down, so soon. Medgar, Malcolm, Martin: and their widows, and their children. Reverend Ralph David Abernathy asked a certain sister to sing a song which Martin had loved— "once more," said Ralph David, "for Martin and for me," and he sat down.

The long, dark sister, whose name I do not remember, rose, very beautiful in her robes, and in her covered grief, and began to sing. It was a song I knew: "My Heavenly Father Watches Over Me." The song rang out as it might have over dark fields, long ago; she was singing of a covenant a people had made, long ago, with life, and with that larger life which ends in revelation and which moves in love.

He guides the eagle through the pathless air.

She stood there, and she sang it. How she bore it, I do not know; I think I have never seen a face quite like that face that afternoon. She was singing it for Martin, and for us.

And surely, He
Remembers me.
My heavenly Father watches over me.

At last, we were standing, and filing out, to walk behind Martin, home. I found myself between Marlon and Sammy.

I had not been aware of the people when I had been pressing past them to get to the church. But, now, as we came out, and I looked up the road, I saw them. They were all along the road, on either side, they were on all the roofs, on either side. Every inch of ground, as far as the eye could see, was black with black people, and they stood in silence. It was the silence that undid me. I started to cry, and I stumbled, and Sammy grabbed my arm. We started to walk.

A week or so later, Billy and I were having a few drinks in some place like The Factory, I think, and one of the young Hollywood producers came over to the table to insist that the Martin Luther King story should be done at once, and that I should write it. I said that I couldn't, because I was tied up with Malcolm. (I also thought that it was a terrible idea, but I didn't bother to say so.)

Well, if I couldn't, what black writer could? He asked me to give him some names, and I did. But he shook his head, finally, and said, No, I was the only one who could do it.

I was still not reacting very quickly. But Billy got mad.

"You don't really mean any of that crap," he said, "about Jimmy being the greatest, and all that. That's bullshit. You mean that Jimmy's a commercial name, and if you get that name on a marquee linked with

Martin Luther King's name, you'll make yourself some bread. That's what *you* mean."

Billy spoke the truth, but it's hard to shame the devil.

————————

In February, the Panthers in Oakland gave a birthday party for the incarcerated Huey Newton. They asked me to "host" this party, and so I flew to Oakland. The birthday party was, of course, a rally to raise money for Huey's defense, and it was a way of letting the world know that the sorely beleaguered Panthers had no intention of throwing in the towel. It was also a way of letting the world—and Huey—know how much they loved and honored the very young man who, along with Bobby Seale, had organized The Black Panther Party for Self Defense, in the spring of 1966. That was the original name of the Party, and the name states very succinctly the need which brought the Party into existence.

It is a need which no black citizen of the ghetto has to have spelled out. When, as white cops are fond of pointing out to me, ghetto citizens "ask for more cops, not less," what they are asking for is more police protection: for crimes committed by blacks against blacks have never been taken very seriously. Furthermore, the prevention of crimes such as these is not the reason for the policeman's presence. That black people need protection *against* the police is indicated by the black community's reaction to the advent of the

Panthers. Without community support, the Panthers would have been merely another insignificant street gang. It was the reaction of the black community which triggered the response of the police: these young men, claiming the right to bear arms, dressed deliberately in guerrilla fashion, standing nearby whenever a black man was accosted by a policeman to inform the black man of his rights and insisting on the right of black people to self defense, were immediately marked as "trouble-makers."

But white people seem affronted by the black distrust of white policemen, and appear to be astonished that a black man, woman, or child can have any reason to fear a white cop. One of the jurors challenged by Charles Garry during the *voir dire* proceedings before Huey's trial had this to say:

"As I said before, that I feel, and it is my opinion that racism, bigotry, and segregation is something that we have to wipe out of our hearts and minds, and not on the street. I have had an opinion that—and been taught never to resist a police officer, that we have courts of law in which to settle—no matter how much I thought I was in the right, the police officer would order me to do something, I would do it expecting if I thought I was right in what I was doing, that I could get justice in the courts"—And, in response to Garry's question, "Assuming the police officer pulled a gun and shot you, what would you do about it?" the prospective juror, at length, replied, "Let me say this. I do not believe a police officer will do that."

This is a fairly vivid and accurate example of the American piety at work. The beginning of the statement is revealing indeed: "——racism, bigotry, and segregation is something we have to wipe out of our hearts and minds and not on the street." One can wonder to whom the "we" here refers, but there isn't any question as to the object of the tense, veiled accusation contained in "not on the street." Whoever the "we" is, it is probably not the speaker—to leave it at that: but the anarchy and danger *"on the street"* are the fault of the blacks. Unnecessarily: for the police are honorable, and the courts are just.

It is no accident that Americans cling to this dream. It involves American self-love on some deep, disastrously adolescent level. And Americans are very carefully and deliberately conditioned to believe this fantasy: by their politicians, by the news they get and the way they read it, by the movies, and the television screen, and by every aspect of the popular culture. If I learned nothing else in Hollywood, I learned how abjectly the purveyors of the popular culture are manipulated. The brainwashing is so thorough that blunt, brutal reality stands not a chance against it; the revelation of corruption in high places, as in the recent "scandals" in New Jersey, for example, has no effect whatever on the American complacency; nor have any of our recent assassinations had any more effect than to cause Americans to arm—thus proving their faith in

the law!—and double-lock their doors. No doubt, behind these locked doors, with their weapons handy,
they switch on the tube and watch The F.B.I., or some
similarly reassuring fable. It means nothing, therefore, to say to so thoroughly insulated a people that
the forces of crime and the forces of law and order
work hand in hand in the ghetto, bleeding it day and
night. It means nothing to say that, in the eyes of the
black and the poor certainly, the principal distinction
between a policeman and a criminal is to be found in
their attire. A criminal can break into one's house
without warning, at will, and harass or molest everyone in the house, and even commit murder, and so can
a cop, and they do; whoever operates whatever hustle
in the ghetto without paying off the cops does not stay
in business long; and it will be remembered—Malcolm
certainly remembered it—that the dope trade flour-
ished in the ghetto for years without ever being seriously molested. Not until white boys and girls began
to be hooked—not until the plague in the ghetto
spread outward, as plagues do—was there any public
uproar. As long as it was only the niggers who were
killing themselves and paying white folks handsomely
for the privilege, the forces of law and order were
silent. The very structure of the ghetto is a nearly
irresistible temptation to criminal activity of one kind
or another: it is a very rare man who does not victimize
the helpless. There is no pressure on the landlord to
be responsible for the upkeep of his property: the only

161

pressure on him is to collect his rent; that is, to bleed the ghetto. There is no pressure on the butcher to be honest: if he can sell bad meat at a profit, why should he not do so? buying cheap and selling dear is what made this country great. If the storekeeper can sell, on the installment plan, a worthless "bedroom suite" for six or seven times its value, what is there to prevent him from doing so, and who will ever hear, or credit, his customer's complaint? in the unlikely event that the customer has any notion of where to go to complain. And the ghetto is a goldmine for the insurance companies. A dime a week, for five or ten or twenty years, is a lot of money, but rare indeed is the funeral paid for by the insurance. I myself do not know of any. Some member of my family had been carrying insurance at a dime a week for years and we finally persuaded her to drop it and cash in the policy—which was now worth a little over two hundred dollars. And let me state candidly, and I know, in this instance, that I do not speak only for myself, that every time I hear the black people of this country referred to as "shiftless" and "lazy," every time it is implied that the blacks deserve their condition here (look at the Irish! look at the Poles! Yes. Look at them.) I think of all the pain and sweat with which these greasy dimes were earned, with what trust they were given, in order to make the difficult passage somewhat easier for the living, in order to show honor to the dead, and I then have no compassion whatever for this country, or my countrymen.

Into this maelstrom, this present elaboration of the slave quarters, this rehearsal for a concentration camp, we place, armed, not for the protection of the ghetto but for the protection of American investments there, some blank American boy who is responsible only to some equally blank elder patriot—Andy Hardy and his pious father. Richard Harris, in his New Yorker article, *The Turning Point*, observes that "Back in 1969, a survey of three hundred police departments around the country had revealed that less than one percent required any college training. Three years later, a pilot study ordered by the President showed that most criminals were mentally below average, which suggested that that policemen who failed to stop or find them might not be much above it."

The white cop in the ghetto is as ignorant as he is frightened, and his entire concept of police work is to cow the natives. He is not compelled to answer to these natives for anything he does; whatever he does, he knows that he will be protected by his brothers, who will allow nothing to stain the honor of the force. When his working day is over, he goes home and sleeps soundly in a bed miles away—miles away from the niggers, for that is the way he really thinks of black people. And he is assured of the rightness of his course and the justice of his bigotry every time Nixon,

163

or Agnew, or Mitchell—or the Governor of the State of California—open their mouths.

Watching the Northern reaction to the Black Panthers, observing the abject cowardice with which the Northern populations allow them to be menaced, jailed, and murdered, and all this with but the faintest pretense to legality, can fill one with great contempt for that emancipated North which, but only yesterday, was so full of admiration and sympathy for the heroic blacks in the South. Luckily, many of us were skeptical of the righteous Northern sympathy then, and so we are not overwhelmed or disappointed now. Luckily, many of us have always known, as one of my brothers put it to me something like twenty-four years ago, that ".the spirit of the South is the spirit of America." Now, exactly like the Germans at the time of the Third Reich, though innocent men are being harassed, jailed, and murdered, in all the Northern cities, the citizens know nothing, and wish to know nothing, of what is happening around them. Yet the advent of the Panthers was as inevitable as the arrival of that day in Montgomery, Alabama, when Mrs. Rosa Parks refused to stand up on that bus and give her seat to a white man. That day had been coming for a very long time; danger upon danger, and humiliation upon humiliation, had piled intolerably high and gave Mrs. Parks her platform. If Mrs. Parks had merely had a headache that day, and if the community had had no grievances, there would have been no bus boycott and so anxious to create work and study programs in the ghetto—everything from hot lunches for school children to academic courses in high schools and colleges to the content, format, and distribution of the Black Panther newspapers. All of these are antidotes to the demoralization which is the scourge of the ghetto, are techniques of self-realization. This is also why they are taught to bear arms—not, like most white Americans, because they fear their neighbors, though indeed they have the most to fear, but in order, this time, to protect *their* lives, *their* women and children, *their* homes, rather than the life and property of an Uncle Sam who has rarely been able to treat his black nephews with more than a vaguely benign contempt. For the necessity, now, which I think nearly all black people see in different ways, is the creation and protection of a nucleus which will bring into existence a new people.

The Black Panthers made themselves visible—made themselves targets, if you like—in order to hip the black community to the presence of a new force in its midst, a force working toward the health and liberation of the community. It was a force which set itself in opposition to that force which uses people as things and which grinds down men and women and children, not only in the ghetto, into an unrecognizable powder. They announced themselves especially as a force for the rehabilitation of the young—the young who were simply perishing, in and out of schools, on the needle, in the Army, or in prison. The black community recog-

Administration," which is of a stunning, unprecedented unanimity. The administration, increasingly, can rule only by fear: the fears of the people who elected them, and the fear that the administration can inspire. In spite of the tear gas, mace, clubs, helicopters, bugged installations, spies, *provocateurs*, tanks, machine guns, prisons, and detention centers, this is a shaky foundation. And they have helped to create a new pantheon of black heroes. Black babies will be born with new names hereafter and will have a standard to which to aspire new in this country, new in the world. The great question is what this will cost. The great effort is to minimize the damage. While I was on the Coast, Eldridge Cleaver and Bobby Seale and David Hilliard were still free, Fred Hampton and Mark Clark were still alive. Now, every day brings a new setback, frequently a bloody one. The government is absolutely determined to wipe the Black Panthers from the face of the earth: which is but another way of saying that it is absolutely determined to keep the nigger in his place. But this merciless and bloody repression, which is carried out, furthermore, with a remarkable contempt for the sensibilities and intelligence of the black people of this nation—for who can believe the police reports?—causes almost all blacks to realize that neither the government, the police, nor the populace are able to distinguish between a Black Panther, a black school child, or a black lawyer. And this reign of terror is creating a great problem in prisons all over this country. "Now, look," said a harassed prison official to Bobby Seale, "you got a lot of notoriety. We don't want no organizing here, or nothing else. We ain't got no Panthers, we ain't got no Rangers, we ain't got no Muslims. All we got is in-mates." All he's got is trouble. All he's got is black people who know why they're in prison, and not all of them can be kept in solitary. These blacks have unforgiving relatives, to say nothing of unforgiving children, at every level of American life. The government cannot afford to trust a single black man in this country, nor can they penetrate any black's disguise, or apprehend how devious and tenacious black patience can be, and any black man that they appear to trust is useless to them, for he will never be trusted by the blacks. It is true that our weapons do not appear to be very formidable, but, then, they never have. Then, as now, our greatest weapon is silence. As black poet Robert E. Hayden puts it in his poem to Harriet Tubman, "Runagate, Runagate": *Mean mean mean to be free.*

I first met Huey in San Francisco, shortly before his fateful encounter with Officers Frey and Heanes. This encounter took place at 5 A.M., in Oakland, on October 28, 1967—on the same day, oddly enough, that Tony Maynard, halfway across the world, was also being arrested for murder.

I had been in San Francisco with my sister, Gloria, I to hide out in a friend's house, working, and she to look after me, and also, poor girl, to rest. It had been a hard, embattled year and we were simply holding our breath, waiting for it to end. We hoped, with that apprehension refugees must feel when they are approaching a border, that the passage would be unnoticeable and that no further disasters would whiten the bleaching year.

A very old friend of mine, a black lady—old in the sense of friendship, indeterminate as to age—made a big West Indian dinner for us in her apartment, and it was also on this evening that I first met Eldridge Cleaver. I'd heard a lot about Cleaver, but all that I knew of Huey Newton was that poster of him in that elaborate chair, as the Black Panthers' Minister of Defense. I talked to him very little that evening. He and Gloria talked, and, as I remember, they scarcely talked to anyone else. I was very impressed by Huey—by his youth, his intelligence, and by a kind of vivid anxiety of hope in him which made his face keep changing as lights failed or flared within. Gloria was impressed by his manners. She had expected, I know, an intolerant, rabble-rousing type who might address her, sneeringly, as "sister," and put her down for not wearing a natural, and give her an interminable, intolerable, and intolerant lecture on the meaning of "black." "I am *tired*," Gloria sometimes said, "of these middle-class, college-educated *darkies* who never saw a rat or a roach in their lives and who never starved or worked a day —who just turned black last *week*—coming and telling *me* what it means to be black." Huey wasn't and isn't like that at all. Huey talks a lot—he has a lot to talk about—but Huey listens.

Anyway, the two of them got on famously. Before we parted, Huey gave me several Black Panther newspapers (the beginning of *my* file on the Panthers, Mr. Mitchell) and he and Eldridge and I promised to keep in touch, and to see each other soon.

I was very much impressed by Eldridge, too—it's impossible not to be impressed by him—but I felt a certain constraint between us. I felt that he didn't like me—or not exactly that: that he considered me a rather doubtful quantity. I'm used to this, though I can't claim to like it. I knew he'd written about me in *Soul On Ice,* but I hadn't yet read it. Naturally, when I did read it, I didn't like what he had to say about me at all. But, eventually—especially as I admired the book, and felt him to be valuable and rare—I thought I could see why he felt impelled to issue what was, in fact, a warning: he was being a zealous watchman on the city wall, and I do not say that with a sneer. He seemed to feel that I was a dangerously odd, badly twisted, and fragile reed, of too much use to the Establishment to be trusted by blacks. I felt that he used my public reputation against me both naïvely and unjustly, and I also felt that I was confused in his mind with the unutterable debasement of the male—with all those faggots, punks, and sissies, the sight and sound of whom, in prison, must have made him vomit more than once. Well, I certainly hope I know more about myself, and the intention of my work than that, but I *am* an odd quantity. So is Eldridge; so are we all. It is a pity that we won't, probably, ever have the time to attempt to define once more the relationship of the odd and disreputable artist to the odd and disreputable revolutionary; for the revolutionary, however odd, is rarely disreputable in the same way that an artist can be. These two seem doomed to stand forever at an odd and rather uncomfortable angle to each other, and they both stand at a sharp and not always comfortable angle to the people they both, in their different fashions, hope to serve. But I think that it is just as well to remember that the people are one mystery and that the person is another. Though I know what a very bitter and delicate and dangerous conundrum this is, it yet seems to me that a failure to respect the person so dangerously limits one's perception of the people that one risks betraying them and oneself, either by sinking to the apathy of cynical disappointment, or rising to the rage of knowing, better than the people do, what the people want. Ultimately, the artist and the revolutionary function as they function, and pay whatever dues they must pay behind it because they are both possessed by a vision, and they do not so much follow this vision as find themselves driven by it. Otherwise, they could never endure, much less embrace, the lives they are compelled to lead. And I think we need each other, and have much to learn from each other, and, more than ever, now.

Huey and I were supposed to meet again one afternoon, but something happened and Huey couldn't make it. Shortly thereafter Gloria and I returned to New York; eventually we received a phone call from a friend, telling us what had happened to Huey. Gloria's reaction was, first—"That nice boy!" and then a sombre, dry, bitter, "At least he isn't dead."

Many months later, I went to see him, with Charles Garry, his lawyer, and some other journalists, in the Alameda County Courthouse. I remember it as being a hot day; the little room in which we sat was very crowded. Huey looked somewhat thinner and paler than when we had first met, but he was very good-natured and lucid.

Huey is a hard man to describe. People surrounded by legend rarely look the parts they've been assigned, but, in Huey's case, the Great Casting Director decided to blow everybody's mind. Huey looks like the cleanest, most scrubbed, most well-bred of adolescents—everybody's favorite baby-sitter. He is old-fashioned in the most remarkable sense, in that he treats everyone with respect, especially his elders. One can see him—almost—a few years hence working quietly for a law firm, say, able but not distinguished, with a pretty wife and a couple of sturdy children, smoking a pipe, living peacefully in a more or less integrated suburb. I say "almost" because the moment one tries to place him in any ordinary, respectable setting something goes wrong with the picture, leaving a space where one had thought to place Huey. There is in him a dedication as gentle as it is unyielding, absolutely single-minded. I began to realize this when I realized that Huey was always listening and always watching. No doubt he can be fooled, he's human, though he certainly can't be fooled easily; but it would be a very great mistake to try to lie to him. Those eyes take in everything, and behind the juvenile smile, he keeps a complicated scoreboard. It has to be complicated. That day, for example, he was dealing with the press, with photographers, with his lawyer, with me, with prison regulations, with his notoriety in the prison, with the latest pronouncements of Police Chief Gain, with the shape of the terror speedily engulfing his friends and co-workers, and he was also, after all, at that moment, standing in the shadow of the gas chamber.

Anyone, under such circumstances, can be pardoned for being rattled or even rude, but Huey was beautiful, and spoke with perfect candor of what was on his mind. Huey believes, and I do, too, in the necessity of establishing a form of socialism in this country —what Bobby Seale would probably call a "Yankee-Doodle type" socialism. This means an indigenous socialism, formed by, and responding to, the real needs of the American people. This is not a doc-

and morale of the child, for the sake of the health and morale of his elders. It may seem nothing to establish a Liberation school, or to insist that all adult Panther members take Political Education classes, but that school, and those classes, can be very potent antidotes to the tranquilizers this country hands out as morality, truth, and history. A needle, or a piece of bread are nothing, but it is very important that all Panther members are forbidden to steal or take even that much from the people: and it changes a person when he concieves of himself, in Huey's words, as "an ox to be ridden by the people." To study the economic structure of this country, to know which hands control the wealth, and to which end, seems an academic exercise —and yet it is necessary, all of it is necessary, for discipline, for knowledge, and for power. Since the blacks are so seriously outnumbered, it is possible to dismiss these passionate exercises as mere acts of faith, preposterous to everyone but the believer: but no one in power appears to find the Panthers even remotely preposterous. On the contrary, they have poured out on these black, defenseless, outnumbered heads a storm of retribution so unspeakably vindictive as to have attracted the wondering and skeptical notice of the world—which does not accept the American version of reality as gospel; and they apparently consider the Panthers so dangerous that nations—or, rather, governments—friendly to the United States have refused to allow individual Panthers to land on their shores, much to the displeasure of their already restive and distinctly crucial student populations. This is to sum up the effect of the Panthers negatively, but this effect reveals volumes about America, and our role in the world. Those who rule in this country now —as distinguished, it must be said, from governing it —are determined to smash the Panthers in order to hide the truth of the American black situation. They want to hide this truth from black people—by making it impossible for them to respond to it—and they would like to hide it from the world; and not, alas, because they are ashamed of it but because they have no intention of changing it. They cannot afford to change it. They would not know how to go about changing it, even if their imaginations were capable of encompassing the concept of black freedom. But this concept lives in their imaginations, and in the popular imagination, only as a nightmare. Blacks have never been free in this country, never was it intended that they should be free, and the spectre of so dreadful a freedom—the idea of a license so bloody and abandoned—conjures up another, unimaginable country, a country in which no decent, God-fearing white man or woman can live. A civilized country is, by definition, a country dominated by whites, in which the blacks clearly know their place. This is really the way the generality of white Americans feel, and they consider —quite rightly, as far as any concern for their interest goes—that it is they who, now, at long last, are being represented in Washington. And, of course, any real commitment to black freedom in this country would have the effect of reordering all our priorities, and altering all our commitments, so that, for horrendous example, we would be supporting black freedom fighters in South Africa and Angola, and would not be allied with Portugal, would be closer to Cuba than we are to Spain, would be supporting the Arab nations instead of Israel, and would never have felt compelled to follow the French into Southeast Asia. But such a course would forever wipe the smile from the face of that friend we all rejoice to have at Chase Manhattan. The course we *are* following is bound to have the same effect, and with dreadful repercussions, but to hint such things now is very close to treason. In spite of our grim situation, and even facing the possibility that the Panthers may be smashed and driven underground, they—that is, the black people here—yet have more going for them than did those outnumbered Christians, running through the catacombs: and digging the grave, as Malcolm put it, of the mighty Roman empire.

In this place, and more particularly, in this time, generations appear to flower, flourish, and wither with the speed of light. I don't think that this is merely the inevitable reflection of middle age: I suspect that there really has been some radical alteration in the structure, the nature, of time. One may say that there are no clear images; everything seems superimposed on, and at war with something else. There are no clear vistas: the road that seems to pull one forward into the future is also pulling one backward into the past. I felt, anyway, kaleidoscopic, fragmented, walking through the streets of San Francisco, trying to decipher whatever it was that my own consciousness made of all the elements in which I was entangled, and which were all tangled up in me. In spite of the fact that my reasons for being in San Francisco were rather chilling, there were compensations. Looking into Huey's face, even though he was in jail, had been a kind of compensation —at least I knew that he was holding on. Talking to Charles Garry, because he is intelligent, honest, and vivid, and devoted to Huey, had been a compensation, and meeting Huey's brother, Melvin, and simply walking through the streets of San Francisco, by far my favorite town—my favorite American town.

I had first been in San Francisco at the height of the civil rights movement, first on an *Esquire* junket, then on a lecture tour. There had been no flower children here then, only earnest, eager students anxious to know what they could "do." Would black people take it amiss if the white kids came into the neighborhood, and—fraternized is probably the only word—with the kids in the pool halls, the bars, the soda fountains? Would black people take is amiss if some of them were to visit a black church? Could they invite members of the black congregation to their white churches, or would the black people feel uncomfortable? Wouldn't it be a good idea if the black and white basketball teams played each other? And there wouldn't be any trouble about the dance afterward, because all the fellows would invite their own dates. Did I think they should go south to work on voting registration this summer, or should they stay home and work in their own communities? Some of them wanted to get a discussion started on open housing—on Proposition Fourteen—and would I come and speak and answer questions? What do you do about older people who are *very nice, really,* but who just—well, who just don't seem to understand the issues—what do you say to them, what do you do? And the black kids: It's another way of life—you have to understand that. *Yeah,* a whole lot of black people are going to put you down, you have to understand *that.* Man, I know my mother don't really want to come to your church. We got more life in *our* church. Mr. B., Brother Malcolm says that no people in history have ever been respected who did not own their own land. What do you say about that, and how are we going to *get* the land? My parents think I shouldn't be sitting in and demonstrating and all that, that I should be getting an education first. What do you think about that? Mr. B., what do you say to an older black man who just feels discouraged about everything? Mr. B., what are we going to do about the dope traffic in the ghetto? Mr. B., do you think black people should join the Army? Mr. B., do you think the Muslims are right and we should be a separate state?

Mr. B., have you ever been to Africa? Mr. B., don't you think the first thing our people need is unity? How can we trust those white people in Washington? they don't really care about black people. Mr. B., what do you think of integration? Don't you think it might just be a trap, to brainwash black people? I come to the conclusion that the man just ain't never going to do right. He a devil, just like Malcolm says he is. I told my teacher I wasn't going to salute the flag no more—don't you think I was right? You mean, if we have a dance after the basketball game, all the brothers is going to have to dance with the *same girl* all night? What about the white guys? Oh, they can dance with *your* girl. Laughter, embarrassment, bewildered ill-feeling. Mr. B., What do *you* think of intermarriage?

Real questions can be absurdly phrased, and probably can be answered only by the questioner, and, at that, only in time. But real questions, especially from the young, are very moving and I will always remember the faces of some of those children. Though the questions facing them were difficult, they appeared, for the most part, to like the challenge. It is true that the white students seemed to look on the black students with some apprehension and some bewilderment, and they also revealed how deeply corrupted they were by the doctrine of white supremacy in many unconscious ways. But the black students, though they were capable of an elaborate, deliberate, and overpowering condescension, seemed, for the most part, to have their tongue in their cheek and exhibited very little malice or venom—toward the students: they felt toward their white elders a passionate contempt.

What seemed most to distress the white students—distress may be too strong a word; what rendered them thoughtful and uneasy—was the unpromising nature of their options. It was not that they had compared their options with those of the black student and been upset by the obvious, worldly injustice. On the contrary, they seemed to feel, some dimly and some desperately, that the roles which they, as whites, were expected to play were not very meaningful, and perhaps—therefore—not very honorable. I remember one boy who was already set to become an executive at one of the major airlines—for him, he joked, bleakly, the sky would be the limit. But he wondered if he could "hold on" to himself, if he could retain the respect of some of the people who respected him now. What he meant was that he hoped not to be programmed out of all meaningful human existence, and, clearly, he feared the worst. He, like many students, was being forced to choose between treason and irrelevance. Their moral obligations to the darker brother, if they were real, and if they were really to be acted on, placed them in conflict with all that they had loved and all that had given them an identity, rendered their present uncertain and their future still more so, and even jeopardized their means of staying alive. They were far from judging or repudiating the

American state as oppressive or immoral—they were merely profoundly uneasy. They were aware that the blacks looked on the white commitment very skeptically indeed, and they made it clear that they did not depend on the whites. They could not depend on the whites until the whites had a clearer sense of what they had let themselves in for. And what the white students had not expected to let themselves in for, when boarding the Freedom Train, was the realization that the black situation in America was but one aspect of the fraudulent nature of American life. They had not expected to be forced to judge their parents, their elders, and their antecedents, so harshly, and they had not realized how cheaply, after all, the rulers of the republic held their white lives to be. Coming to the defense of the rejected and destitute, they were confronted with the extent of their own alienation, and the unimaginable dimensions of their own poverty. They were privileged and secure only so long as they did, in effect, what they were told: but they had been raised to believe that they were free.

I next came to San Francisco at the time of the flower children, when everyone, young and not so young, was freaking out on whatever came to hand. The flower children were all up and down the Haight-Ashbury section of San Francisco—and they might have been everywhere else, too, but for the vigilance of the cops—with their long hair, their beads, their robes, their fancied resistance, and, in spite of a shrewd, hard skepticism as unnerving as it was unanswerable, really tormented by the hope of love. The fact that their uniforms and their jargon precisely represented the distances they had yet to cover before arriving at that maturity which makes love possible—or no longer possible—could not be considered their fault. They had been born into a society in which nothing was harder to achieve, in which perhaps nothing was more scorned and feared than the idea of the soul's maturity. Their flowers had the validity, at least, of existing in direct challenge to the romance of the gun; their gentleness, however specious, was nevertheless a direct repudiation of the American adoration of violence. Yet they looked—alas—doomed. They seemed to sense their doom. They really were flower children, having opted out on the promises and possibilities offered them by the shining and now visibly perishing republic. I could not help feeling, watching them, knowing them to be idealistic, fragmented, and impotent, that, exactly as the Third Reich had had first to conquer the German opposition before getting around to the Jews, and then the rest of Europe, my republic, which, unhappily, I was beginning to think of as the Fourth Reich, would be forced to plow under the flower children—in all their variations—before getting around to the blacks and then the rest of the world.

The blacks, for the most part, were not to be found with the flower children. In the eerie American way, they walked the same streets, were to be found in the same neighborhoods, were the targets of the very same forces, seemed to bear each other no ill will—on the contrary indeed, especially from the point of view of the forces watching them—and yet they seemed to have no effect on each other, and they certainly were not together. The blacks were not putting their trust in flowers. They were putting their trust in guns.

An historical wheel had come full circle. The descendants of the cowboys, who had slaughtered the Indians, the issue of those adventurers who had enslaved the blacks, wished to lay down their swords and shields. But these could be laid down only at Sambo's feet, and this was why they could not be together: I felt like a lip-reader watching the communication of despair.

It was appalling, anyway, with or without flowers, to find so many children in the streets. In benighted, incompetent Africa, I had never encountered an orphan: the American streets resembled nothing so much as one vast, howling, unprecedented orphanage. It has been vivid to me for many years that what we call a race problem here is not a race problem at all: to keep calling it that is a way of avoiding the problem. The problem is rooted in the question of how one treats one's flesh and blood, especially one's children. The blacks are the despised and slaughtered children of the great Western house—nameless and unnameable bastards. This is a fact so obvious, so speedily verifiable, that it would seem pure insanity to deny it, and yet the life of the entire country is predicated on this denial, this monstrous and pathetic lie. For many generations, many a white American has gone—sometimes shrieking—to his grave, knowing that his own son, the issue of his loins, was denied, and sometimes murdered by him. Many a white American woman has gone through life carrying the knowledge that she is responsible for the slaughter of her lover, and also for the destruction of that love's issue. *Ye are liars and the truth's not in you:* it cannot be pretty to be forced, with every day the good Lord sends, to tell so many lies about everything. It demands a tremendous effort of the will and an absolute surrender of the personality to act on the lies one tells oneself. It is not true that people become liars without knowing it. A liar always knows he is lying, and that is why liars travel in packs: in order to be reassured that the judgment day will never come for them. They need each other for the well-being, the health, the perpetuation of their lie. They have a tacit agreement to guard each other's secrets, for they have the same secret. That is why all liars are cruel and filthy minded—one's merely got to listen to their dirty jokes, to what they think is funny, which is also what they think is real.

The flower children seemed completely aware that the blacks were their denied brothers, seemed even to be patiently waiting for the blacks to recognize that they had repudiated the house. For it seemed to have eyes seemed to say, *I didn't do it! Let me pass!* and in such a moment one recognized the fraudulent and expedient nature of the American innocence which has always been able to persuade itself that it does not know what it knows too well. Or, it was exactly like watching someone who finds himself caught in a lie: for a black man abroad is no longer one of "our" niggers, is a stranger, not to be controlled by anything his countrymen think or say or do. In a word, he is free and thus discovers how little equipped his countrymen are to behold him in that state. In San Francisco, the eyes that watched seemed to feel that the children were deliberately giving away family secrets in the hope of egging on the blacks to destroy the family. And that is precisely what they *were* doing—helplessly, unconsciously, out of a profound desire to be saved, to live. But the blacks already knew the family secrets and had no interest in them. Nor did they have much confidence in these troubled white boys and girls. The black trouble was of a different order, and blacks had to be concerned with much more than their own private happiness or unhappiness. They had to be aware that this troubled white person might suddenly decide not to be in trouble and go home—and when he went home, he would be the enemy. Therefore, it was best not to speak too freely to anyone who spoke too freely to you, especially not on the streets of a nation which probably has more hired informers working for it, here and all over the world, than any nation in history.

challenges anyone alive can face—this is what the blacks are saying. Nothing is easier, nor, for the guilt-ridden American, more inevitable, than to dismiss this as chauvinism in reverse. But, in this, white Americans are being—it is a part of their fate—inaccurate. To be liberated from the stigma of blackness by embracing it is to cease, forever, one's interior agreement and collaboration with the authors of one's degradation. It abruptly reduces the white enemy to a contest merely physical, which he can win only physically. White men have killed black men for refusing to say, "Sir": but it was the corroboration of their worth and their power that they wanted, and not the corpse, still less the staining blood. When the black man's mind is no longer controlled by the white man's fantasies, a new balance or what may be described as an unprecedented inequality begins to make itself felt: for the white man no longer knows who he is, whereas the black man knows them both. For if it is difficult to be released from the stigma of blackness, it is clearly at least equally difficult to surmount the delusion of whiteness. And as the black glories in his newfound color, which is *his* at last, and asserts, not always with the very greatest politeness, the unanswerable validity and power of his being—even in the shadow of death —the white is very often affronted and very often made afraid. He has his reasons, after all, not only for being weary of the entire concept of color, but fearful as to what may be made of this concept once it has fallen, as it were, into the wrong hands. And one may indeed be wary, but the point is that it was inevitable that black and white should arrive at this dizzying height of tension. Only when we have passed this moment will we know what our history has made of us.

Many white people appear to live in a state of carefully repressed terror in relation to blacks. There is something curious and paradoxical about this terror, which is involved not only with the common fear of death, but with a sense of its being considered utterly irrelevant whether one is breathing or not. I think that this has something to do with the fact that, whereas white men have killed black men for sport, or out of terror or out of the intolerable excess of terror called hatred, or out of the necessity of affirming their identity as white men, none of these motives appear necessarily to obtain for black men: it is not necessary for a black man to hate a white man, or to have any particular feelings about him at all, in order to realize that he must kill him. Yes, we have come, or are coming to this, and there is no point in flinching before the prospect of this exceedingly cool species of fratricide—which prospect white people, after all, have brought on themselves. Of course, whenever a black man discusses violence he is said to be "advocating" it. This is very far indeed from my intention, if only because I have no desire whatever to see a generation perish in the streets. But the shape and extent of whatever violence may come is not in the hands of people like myself, but in the hands of the American people, who are at present among the most dishonorable and violent people in the world. I am merely trying to face certain blunt, human facts. I do not carry a gun and do not consider myself to be a violent man: but my life has more than once depended on the gun in a brother's holster. I know that when certain powerful and blatant enemies of black people are shoveled, at last, into the ground I may feel a certain pity that they spent their lives so badly, but I certainly do not mourn their passing, nor, when I hear that they are ailing, do I pray for their recovery. I know what I would do if I had a gun and someone had a gun pointed at my brother, and I would not count ten to do it and there would be no hatred in it, nor any remorse. People who treat other people as less than human must not be surprised when the bread they have cast on the waters comes floating back to them, poisoned.

I'm black and I'm proud: yet, I suppose that the most accurate term, now, for this history, this particular and peculiar danger, as well as for all persons produced out of it and struggling in it, is: Afro-American. Which is but a wedding, however, of two confusions, an arbitrary linking of two undefined and currently undefineable proper nouns. I mean that, in the case of Africa, Africa is still chained to Europe, and exploited by Europe, and Europe and America are chained together; and as long as this is so, it is hard to speak of Africa except as a cradle and a potential. Not until the many millions of people on the continent of Africa control their land and their resources will the African personality flower or genuinely African institutions flourish and reveal Africa as she is. But it is striking that that part of the North American continent which calls itself, arrogantly enough, *America* poses as profound and dangerous a mystery for human understanding as does the fabled dark continent of Africa. The terms in which the mystery is posed, as well as the mysteries themselves, are very different. Yet, when one places the mysteries side by side—ponders the history and possible future of Africa, and the history and possible future of America—something is illuminated of the nature, the depth and the tenacity of the great war between black and white life styles here. Something is suggested of the nature of fecundity, the nature of sterility, and one realizes that it is by no means a simple matter to know which is which: the one can very easily resemble the other. Questions louder than drums begin beating in the mind, and one realizes that what is called civilization lives first of all in the mind, has the mind above all as its province, and that the civilization, or its rudiments, can continue to live long after its externals have vanished—they can never entirely vanish from the mind. These questions—they are too vague for questions, this excitement, this discomfort—concern the true nature of any inheritance and the means by which that inheritance is handed down. There is a reason, after all, that some people

193

wish to colonize the moon, and others dance before it as before an ancient friend. And the extent to which these apprehensions, instincts, relations, are modified by the passage of time, or the accumulation of inventions, is a question that no one seems able to answer. All men, clearly, are primitive, but it can be doubted that all men are primitive in the same way; and if they are not, it can only be because, in that absolutely unassailable privacy of the soul, they do not worship the same gods. Both continents, Africa and America, be it remembered, were "discovered"—what a wealth of arrogance that little word contains!—with devastating results for the indigenous populations, whose only human use thereafter was as the source of capital for white people. On both continents the white and the dark gods met in combat, and it is on the outcome of this combat that the future of both continents depends.

To be an Afro-American, or an American black, is to be in the situation, intolerably exaggerated, of all those who have ever found themselves part of a civilization which they could in no wise honorably defend —which they were compelled, indeed, endlessly to attack and condemn—and who yet spoke out of the most passionate love, hoping to make the kingdom new, to make it honorable and worthy of life. Whoever is part of whatever civilization helplessly loves some aspects of it, and some of the people in it. A person does not lightly elect to oppose his society. One would much rather be at home among one's compatriots than be mocked and detested by them. And there is a level on which the mockery of the people, even their hatred, is moving because it is so blind: it is terrible to watch people cling to their captivity and insist on their own destruction. I think black people have always felt this about America, and Americans, and have always seen, spinning above the thoughtless American head, the shape of the wrath to come.

epilogue

WHO HAS BELIEVED OUR REPORT?

This book has been much delayed by trials, assassinations, funerals, and despair. Nor is the American crisis, which is part of a global, historical crisis, likely to resolve itself soon. An old world is dying, and a new one, kicking in the belly of its mother, time, announces that it is ready to be born. This birth will not be easy, and many of us are doomed to discover that we are exceedingly clumsy midwives. No matter, so long as we accept that our responsibility is to the newborn: the acceptance of responsibility contains the key to the necessarily evolving skill.

This book is not finished—can never be finished, by me. As of this writing, I am waiting to hear the fate of Tony Maynard, whose last address was Attica. Though the cops have been buried, with much patriotic grief, the blacks are still waiting to hear who is alive or dead. Mr. Nixon has congratulated Mr. Rockefeller, who has congratulated the police: so much for that. As to the effect of all this—and so much more!—on the Black Panther leadership and on black or non-white people, in this country, and all over the world, time will give a sufficiently authoritative answer. People, even if they are so thoughtless as to be born black, do not come into this world merely to provide mink coats and diamonds for chattering, trivial, pale matrons, or genocidal opportunities for their unsexed, unloved, and, finally, despicable men—oh, pioneers!

There will be bloody holding actions all over the world, for years to come: but the Western party is over, and the white man's sun has set. Period.

Angela Davis is still in danger. George Jackson has joined his beloved baby brother, Jon, in the royal fellowship of death. And one may say that Mrs. Georgia Jackson and the alleged mother of God have, at last, found something in common. Now, it is the Virgin, the alabaster Mary, who must embrace the despised black mother whose children are also the issue of the Holy Ghost.

New York, San Francisco, Hollywood, London, Istanbul, St. Paul de Vence,
1967–1971.

I AM NOT YOUR NEGRO

*A Companion Edition to the Documentary Film Directed
by Raoul Peck*

To compose his stunning documentary film *I Am Not Your
Negro*, acclaimed filmmaker Raoul Peck mined James
Baldwin's published and unpublished oeuvre, selecting
passages from his books, essays, letters, notes, and inter-
views that are every bit as incisive and pertinent now as
they have ever been. Weaving these texts together, Peck
brilliantly imagines the book that Baldwin never wrote. In
his final years, Baldwin had envisioned a book about his
three assassinated friends, Medgar Evers, Malcolm X, and
Martin Luther King, Jr. His deeply personal notes for the
project have never before been published. Peck's film uses
them to jump through time, juxtaposing Baldwin's private
words with his public statements in a blazing examination
of the tragic history of race in America.

Literature

GO TELL IT ON THE MOUNTAIN

Go Tell It on the Mountain, originally published in 1953,
is Baldwin's first major work, a novel that has established
itself as an American classic. With lyrical precision, psycho-
logical directness, resonating symbolic power, and a rage
that is at once unrelenting and compassionate, Baldwin
chronicles a fourteen-year-old boy's discovery one Saturday
in March 1935 of the terms of his identity as the stepson of
the minister of a Pentecostal storefront church in Harlem.
Baldwin's rendering of his protagonist's spiritual, sexual,
and moral struggle toward self-invention opened new possibilities in the American language and in the way Americans
understand themselves.

Fiction

Baldwin's personal reflections on movies gathered here in a book-length essay are also a probing appraisal of American racial politics. Offering an incisive look at racism in American movies and a vision of America's self-delusions and deceptions, Baldwin challenges the underlying assumptions in such films as *In the Heat of the Night*, *Guess Who's Coming to Dinner*, and *The Exorcist*. Here are our loves and hates, biases and cruelties, fears and ignorance reflected by the films that have entertained us and shaped our consciousness. *The Devil Finds Work* showcases the stunning prose of a writer whose passion never diminished his struggle for equality, justice, and social change.

Fiction

ALSO AVAILABLE

The Amen Corner

Another Country

Blues for Mister Charlie

The Cross of Redemption

The Fire Next Time

Giovanni's Room

Going to Meet the Man

If Beale Street Could Talk

Nobody Knows My Name

One Day When I Was Lost

Tell Me How Long the Train's Been Gone

Vintage Baldwin